ZeNLP

the power to succeed

What the PRESS says about ZeNLP

ZeNLP is not going to be written off easily
    —Business & Political Observer

ZeNLP guides a person to achieving his goal
    —Times of India

ZeNLP can also help develop a particular mental attitude
    —Indian Express

ZeNLP can help a lot by energising your mind power
    —Deccan Herald

Managers who have attended ZeNLP programmes are already feeling the difference
    —Asian Age

Over 2500 people have benefited from ZeNLP workshops in the last three years
    —Business Line

ZeNLP works through visualisation techniques and auto-suggestions
    —Hindu

ZeNLP

the power to succeed

murli menon

Response Books
A division of Sage Publications
New Delhi/Thousand Oaks/London

First published in 2004 by

Response Books
A division of Sage Publications India Pvt Ltd
B–42, Panchsheel Enclave
New Delhi – 110 017

Sage Publications Inc	**Sage Publications Ltd**
2455 Teller Road	1 Oliver's Yard
Thousand Oaks	55 City Road
California 91320	London EC1Y 1SP

Published by Tejeshwar Singh for Response Books, typeset in 11.5 pt. AGaramond by InoSoft Systems and printed at Chaman Enterprises, New Delhi.

Third printing 2005

Library of Congress Cataloging-in-Publication Data

Menon, Murli.
    ZeNLP : the power to succeed / Murli Menon.
        p. cm.
    Includes bibliographical references.
    1. Neurolinguistic programming. 2. Meditation—Zen Buddhism.
    3. Kuònòdalinåi. 4. Management—Psychological aspects.
    5. Success—Psychological aspects. I. Title

    BF637.N46M46   2004   158.1—dc22   2004004550

ISBN: 0-7619-9641-9 (US-PB)   81-7829-220-3 (India-PB)

Production Team: Gargi Dasgupta, R.A.M. Brown and Santosh Rawat

For
Deepika, my wife...

I owe this book to you. Without your constant support and encouragement, this book could never have seen the light of the day...

A very special thank you for helping me maintain the ZeNLP vegan diet and for being such a great cook. I only wish that my writing is as good as your cooking.

This book has been energised by your vegetarian delicacies cooked without knowingly using any egg or egg products, milk or milk products and without using any product of animal origin.

Thanks for helping me maintain my dream diary and meditation schedules over the years. Thanks *chotu,* for your patience and for holding on during the hardest and most difficult of times.

contents

list of abbreviations

NLP	Neuro Linguistic Programming
ZeNLP	Neuro Linguistic Programming with a touch of Zen meditation
DHE	Designer Human Engineering
PNI	Psycho-neuro immunology
RAM	Random Access Memory

preface

This book has the potential to change your life. What you are about to read has changed my life. January 1, 1995 was the day my life changed. While returning home after a New Year party, I was hit by a truck. The head-on collision resulted in brain haemorrhage, paralysing the left side of my body. No doctor was brave enough to predict my returning to normalcy. I was destined to live life in bed, if not in a wheelchair. There was severe organic damage to the front temporal lobe of my brain. The subsequent surgical interventions meant total dependency on powerful anti-epileptic drugs for the rest of my life. But the doctors did not know about ZeNLP. I had undergone advanced training in NLP (Neuro Linguistic Programming) and was practising Zen meditation regularly before my accident. I knew that mind power could cure any disease including epilepsy, paralysis and cancer.

All that was needed was to have a goal and effectively programme my mind though NLP techniques to reach my goal. Being an invalid and restricted to bed due to my injuries and having the luxury of ample time to visualise, chant and meditate, I orchestrated my own recovery without the use of allopathic, homeopathic, herbal or ayurvedic medicines. In the last nine years, I have not had a single epileptic attack due to my immense faith in the power of the human mind. ZeNLP says one can programme the mind through meditation and visualisation, one can programme the body through diet, fasting and exercise, and one can programme the soul through prayers and chanting.

In the last nine years, my experience has empowered many other unfortunate victims of fate to overcome their disabilities through tribal meditation, visualisation, auto-suggestion and NLP. I recovered full use of both my limbs by June 1995 and, over the last six years, conducted several workshops all over India and abroad on goal setting and achievement, stress management, team-building and motivation based on ZeNLP. We have opened up the minds of thousands of participants who have attended our workshops from corporate board-rooms to schools to hospitals.

We set goals and marched relentlessly towards them with single minded determination: By combining NLP visualisations with meditation, by disciplining the body through fasting and by disciplining the soul through prayers and chanting. One can use the principles of ZeNLP to create lasting and permanent change. ZeNLP guides managers to individual and organisational goals by harnessing the infinite power of their minds.

acknowledgements

I have learnt the lesson to write this book from all human beings I interacted with after taking birth on planet earth. I have also gained knowledge from the collective consciousness of humanity. Hence I thank all 6 billion human beings on planet earth who have contributed to my book.

However, I must say special thanks to Mr Tejeshwar Singh of Sage Publications for publishing this book. I would also like to acknowledge the silent motivation provided to me by N.V. Ramanand, B.K. Satpathy, Rashida Bhagat, R.K. Mattoo, Prashant Sahu, Reema Moudgal, Shyam Hari Chakra, Debdas Thakur, Debrata Mohanty and Radhika, Tarun Joshi, Sarala Hombali, B.P. Mohapatra, V. Muthiah, Ashok Tandon, P.V. Ramachandran, Ranjan Kaul, Anil Chandy, Chapal Mehra, Rasheed Kappan and Satyamurthy. I am thankful for the great effort put in by the production team which includes Richard Brown, Gargi Dasgupta and Santosh Rawat.

I would also like to acknowledge the support of Ashima Sahu (Nani), Honeynani and Rubynani (during my stay at Bhubaneshwar). Above all, I am indebted to my father Kannanunni Menon, mother Sowbhagyawati Menon, sisters Priya and Prasanna, Dr. Gangadhar Sahu and Ashalata Sahu for their continued support and helping me follow the ZeNLP diet, since January'1997.

Meditation is verily greater than intelligence. The earth meditates as it were. The water meditates as it were. The sun meditates as it were. Therefore, those who attain greatness among men have attained benefit of meditation as it were

— Chandogya Upanishad 6.1

Mind is the reason for liberation and mind is the reason for bondage

— Shreemad Bhagavad Geeta (600 B.C.)

chapter 1

introduction to cosmic consciousness

Theoretically, the human body is made up of trillions of cells. These cells are chemical in nature and are composed of molecules of Carbon, Nitrogen, Oxygen and Hydrogen in various combinations. If these molecules are viewed through an electron microscope, they are made up of atoms which can further be divided into electrons, neutrons and protons. Neutrons can further be divided into neutrinos. But the tiniest particle of an atom can be smashed into is a quark. Quarks are quantum energy. Thus, the human body is only a bundle of energy.

Experiences of the human race are all expressions of energy. As energy can neither be created nor destroyed, these experiences are stored in the cosmos and have been termed as 'cosmic consciousness' by psychologists. A few psychologists including Carl Gustave Jung have spent a large part of their lives trying to scientifically validate the existence of cosmic consciousness.

Scientific thinking has been imprisoned by the theory of relativity, which says that matter cannot move faster than the speed of light. However, the theory of cosmic consciousness predates the theory of relativity by 5000 years as explained in this Rig Vedic mantra.

Om Poornamidam Poornat Poornamudachyate
Poornasya Poornamadaya Poornamevavashisyate

This mantra means that the macrocosm is contained in the microcosm. We split the atom and see electrons and protons revolving around a nucleus, which is but a reflection of the planets revolving around the sun. Thus, the macrocosm (universe) is contained in the microcosm (atom). All events in the macrocosm can be predicted with certainty if one understands the cosmic mind after the awakening of the cosmic consciousness.

The best part of cosmic consciousness is that all human beings are equally capable of realising their consciousness by a simple spiritual regimen irrespective of religious beliefs. Such practices, visualisation, auto-suggestion and meditations are suggested at ZeNLP workshops conducted by us. Since October 1995, when we started conducting workshops to awaken cosmic consciousness, more than 3500 participants have experienced their inner power.

Today, websites on spirituality and spiritual consciousness receive millions of hits per day and we receive more than 100 emails every month from America, Europe and South Africa requesting more information on the process of awakening cosmic consciousness. Some scholar has rightly said, *The multitude of books is making us ignorant*. Carlos Casteneda, the great anthropologist who spent decades researching the traditions of the Yakui Indians in Mexico and studied their shamanic ceremonies, wrote a series of books on Yakui Indian dream ceremonies. These ceremonies were similar to those practised by Indian sages and ascetics since Vedic times.

A detailed analysis of ancient rituals of indigenous tribes all over the world reveals amazing results. Rituals to awaken cosmic consciousness were found among Mayans (America), Incas (Peru), Hopi Indians (America), Dang tribals (Gujarat), Simlipal tribals (Orissa), Gonds (Madhya Pradesh), Bhils (Maharashtra), Soligas (Karnataka), Yakui Indians (Mexico), Zen Buddhists (Japan), Gorkhas (Nepal) and the Tibetan Lamas. The Falun Gong movement in China also attempts to tap this cosmic energy through a regimen of meditation, diet and exercise.

These rituals are the same across countries around the globe and among tribes that had no physical contact with each other. The mysteries of construction of giant pyramids in countries as scattered as Egypt, Peru and Mexico also point to a shared knowledge among the ancients, which points to the fact that these civilisations could draw upon cosmic consciousness far early in their evolution. As most practices to awaken cosmic consciousness have been passed on by tribals over generations, without the existence of written records, only few documented sources are available to mankind to re-establish contact with cosmic consciousness.

The most prominent among them are the Vedas. Vedic literature has propounded the theory of cosmic energy over 5000 years and most yogic practices including *kriya yoga, sankya yoga, hatha yoga, siddha yoga, karma yoga* and *bhakti yoga* are pathways to reach cosmic awakening.

Cosmic consciousness has three phases: Creation, Maintenance and Dissolution represented by *satva, rajas* and *tamas* respectively. In scientific terms, this consciousness represents the infinite potential energy stored in the human brain that can be activated by disciplining the body through fasting, mind through meditation, and soul through prayer.

In yoga, cosmic consciousness is closely allied with the concept of kundalini—*kunda* which means coiled and *lini* meaning energy—which is symbolised as a serpent coiled up three and a half times and residing at the base of the spine at the tailbone or coccyx. This is the dormant phase of kundalini.

When kundalini is awakened, it moves through the seven chakras represented in the gross human body as *muladhara* (spine), *swadisthana* (pelvis), *manipura* (navel), *anahata* (heart), *visshudha* (throat), *ajnya* (forehead) and *sahasra* (crown). When the energy liberated from the coccyx traverses these seven chakras and strikes the pineal gland situated in the brain, cosmic consciousness is awakened.

The release of cosmic consciousness is such an intense and pleasurable experience that those who have experienced it would like to prolong the experience indefinitely. However, the awakening should always be undertaken under special guidance as the body, mind and soul must be prepared to experience this high voltage energy. There have been instances of spontaneous human combustion (where the human body ignites spontaneously leaving charred remains) which have been attributed to awakening cosmic consciousness among alcoholics, smokers and excessive red-meat eaters. The awakening of cosmic consciousness among alcoholics, smokers, non-vegans (vegans do not eat meat, fish, eggs, milk or any milk products) can have disastrous physical and psychological consequences. Here it is important to mention the fact that every year one million Americans are turning vegan and it is not difficult to find vegan eateries even in far-flung US states.

Spontaneous awakening of cosmic consciousness can occur during surgery, accidents or during frenzied activities like attending rock concerts, watching freestyle wrestling or taking part in any group activity that generates mass hysteria. However, as the body is not prepared to receive this high-voltage energy, it can result in psychological imbalances.

There are physical, psychological and spiritual benefits of awakening cosmic consciousness through meditation. The first and foremost is the ability to be energetic and active irrespective of your physical age. You become a source of boundless physical energy. Individuals with health problems become spontaneously healed once this *adi-parashakti* (tribal word meaning ancient, powerful energy or cosmic energy or primordial power) is awakened. This explains why certain people with cancer succumb to the disease while others continue to live. It also explains why certain patients are cured of paralysis while others continue to be bedridden for decades. Weight becomes steady. Individuals who awaken their cosmic consciousness start losing weight spontaneously and reach the ideal body weight needed for their height and continue to stay at the level for decades. Hair loss and greying are reversed and the skin becomes more radiant and youthful. Individuals who are able to awaken their cosmic consciousness are characterised by a calm and serene face, congruence of body movement, soft speech and a sense of peace when alone. A photographic memory, improved concentration and super reading speeds are some of the other benefits that accrue to such awakened minds.

In exceptional cases where the awakening is to a very advanced degree, the power of prophecy (predicting events before they actually happen) is bestowed upon the awakened individual. Cosmic consciousness or the cosmic mind is the collective consciousness of every single electron, atom and molecule that exists in this infinite universe. The secrets of the universe are revealed to awakened individuals through the cosmic mind.

Cosmic consciousness can be awakened fully or partially through a combination of physical exercises (yoga), controlled breathing (*pranayama*), meditation, chanting and prayer. The objective of this book is to introduce managers to spiritual practices that can enhance their personal and team effectiveness. ZeNLP is a combination of techniques to connect to cosmic consciousness. It attempts to explore the unknown and enhance managerial effectiveness through unconventional techniques like dream analysis.

Cosmic consciousness can be activated through the discipline of mind, body and soul. Discipline of mind can be achieved through meditation. The body can be disciplined through exercise and fasting. The soul can be disciplined through total surrender and prayer. This surrender could be to God or to the cosmic force, Mother Nature, primordial force or elemental energy.

This book is a collection of articles with a loose common thread that binds chapters which seem unconnected. However, one finds a mysterious force which guides you to discover the hidden connections between the various chapters and awakens your intuitive powers to give you a holistic view of the sequence of activities needed to be co-ordinated in order to benefit from the techniques elucidated in this book.

Learning management through metaphors is fun and makes learning enjoyable. A successful manager has to be a capable leader, a team-player, effective in delegating authority and responsibility to subordinates, a good communicator and much much more. However, budding management trainees should imbibe these qualities unconsciously during the course of your education and training to complete the metamorphosis into successful managers.

One day, a monk asks a woodcutter, who is hacking away at the tree, 'How many hours do you need to cut a tree?' 'Four hours', replies the woodcutter. 'And how do you cut a tree in four hours?' repeats the monk. 'I sharpen my axe for the first three hours and cutting the tree takes me only an hour'.

Training, both on the job and through technical as well as management development workshops, do play an important role in the moulding of successful managers. Practising managers have to constantly strive to sharpen their axes so that they can be more effective and efficient in their designated role. In the forthcoming chapters, essential and managerial qualities are elucidated through the use of metaphors from the animal kingdom. These metaphors help one to get a better understanding of the essential managerial qualities needed to manage successfully.

Close observation of nature can provide insights into the finer aspects of management, without having to rely on esoteric theories or on packaged truths. Observing nature, can open your eyes to hidden truths and you begin to imbibe the essential managerial qualities needed to be developed to become a successful manager. Observations of behaviour of animals and birds as diverse as penguins, owls, dolphins, and ants show amazing similarities when it comes to essential managerial qualities which play an important role in their survival as a species and their evolutionary progress.

In the last few chapters of this book we take real life examples from the lives of our feathered friends and correlate their experiences to get an indepth look into the essential managerial qualities needed to be imbibed by managers across functional areas, age groups and nationality.

The spiritual practices—diet, exercises and meditation—contained in this book cannot be scientifically explained or validated through clinical trials. However, the benefits of adopting a vegetarian diet, relaxation, meditation and yogic exercises are indisputable. Managers who have learnt and included these practices into their daily regimen have experienced remarkable physical, mental and spiritual benefits.

Most of the techniques elucidated in this book have been practised by me since 1995. Having experienced the benefits of these ancient practices, I would like to share the same with all individuals who would like to improve their personal effectiveness through spiritual empowerment.

Over the years, kundalini has incorrectly been associated with *tantra* and sex, and this has resulted in a lot of misconceptions which have prevented young and educated individuals from exploring their own consciousness. It is an enlightening experience and more and more people should devote time and energy to find out who they really are. This book is a small step in that direction. How will you use this book? The answer to this important question is included in a little story.

One day a child goes to his mother and asks her, 'Ma, who is that old man sitting on the mountain?' Mother answers, 'Don't call him an old man, for he is Lord Buddha, who knows the answer to every question in this universe.' 'Really, he knows answers to all questions?' asks the child. 'Yes, my dear,' replies the mother. The child goes to the mountain where Buddha is meditating, catches a butterfly from the garden, and cupping the butterfly gently in his hands, he approaches Buddha.

Keeping his hand behind his back, he asks Buddha? 'Is the thing in my hand alive or dead?' The child thinks that if Buddha answers that the thing is alive, he will crush the butterfly in his hand and show the dead butterfly proving Buddha wrong. And if Buddha answers that the thing is dead, he will open his gently cupped hand, allowing the butterfly to fly away showing that the butterfly was alive, again proving Buddha wrong. Thus, Buddha did not know the answer to all questions. 'Is the thing in my hand alive or dead?' repeats the eager child. The Buddha opens his eyes, nods his head and replies, 'My dear son, the answer lies in your hands!'

chapter 2

ZeNLP—software for the brain!

ZeNLP is a combination of Zen plus NLP. The history of the word *Zen* is interesting. Zen means meditation or improvement. The word *dhyana* means meditation in Sanskrit and *dhyana* yoga (yoga through the path of meditation) is a part of the Holy Gita. Zen was rooted in China by Bodhidharma who came from India in the sixth century and later carried forward to Japan by the 12th century. *Dhyana* was mispronounced by Chinese monks as *ch'an*, due to their inability to pronounce the Sanskrit word *Dha*. *Ch'an* became *zh'an* in Japan, as the Japanese mispronounced *cha* as *zha*. The modern word Zen, is a descendant of the 12th century Japanese word *zh'an* which meant meditation. Thus, in ZeNLP, Zen is derived from *dhyana*. Thus, ZeNLP has its roots in the Gita, which itself is Lord Krishna's commentary on the Vedas.

ZeNLP or Neuro Linguistic Programming with a touch of meditation is the new technology of achievement. The origins of ZeNLP can be traced back to the Rig Veda—one of India's ancient texts. Taking advantage of the giant strides made in the fields of computer technology, automated translation and digital cameras, our ancient texts have become the focus of in-depth research by western scientists who are rediscovering most of their discoveries, in our ancient scriptures. PNI(Psycho-Neuro-Immunology), which is one of the most recent discoveries in the fields of psychotherapy and immunology, has been discussed in intricate detail in *charaka samhita*. Similarly, NLP has been practised by our 'rishis' since Vedic times and several Vedic *shlokas* talk about the 'mind-body' connection. But Western scientists have done a good job of restructuring our ancient texts into 'acronyms' like PNI and DHE (Designer Human Engineering).

In NLP, neuro is derived from nerves, which represents behaviour. Linguistic is derived from language, which means structure and programming is borrowed from computers, which means creating change. Thus, ZeNLP creates structured behavioural changes in attitudes of individuals whom you communicate with. ZeNLP improves conceptual skills, analytical ability and communication skills of teams, with a focus on body language and communicating with the unconscious.

NLP was created by psychotherapist John Grinder, mathematician and psychologist Richard Bandler in association with Dr Milton H. Erikson, a leading hypnotherapist. Bandler and Grinder have since split and are separately teaching their own versions of NLP to their respective students. NLP originated in the research labs of the University of California at Santa Cruz, and evolved as late as the 1990s.

The computer was modelled on the human brain by its inventor Charles Babbage. The human brain is the most powerful supercomputer in the world, notwithstanding Gary Kasparov's much publicised loss to IBM's Chess-playing computer Deep Blue.

The human brain is a powerful supercomputer. Supercomputers can be programmed by software programs. So, applying deductive logic, the human brain too can be programmed using software! ZeNLP is this software.

As Patanjali's *yoga sutra* elaborates, 'The mind and body are parts of the same system'. Hence, far-reaching changes can be brought about in human behaviour by upgrading our mental software. These changes are permanent and can be brought about by ZeNLP exercises lasting no more than two minutes! I have come across several cases of men and women with phobias, who have overcome their fears, after a few, simple ZeNLP sessions. Just as today's Pentium laptops are more powerful than the gigantic computers of the yesteryears, similarly, a few hours of ZeNLP therapy can cure severe phobias, which conventional psychotherapists used to take months to cure, in the past. Speaking from experience, I overcame paralysis by practising ZeNLP therapy.

ZeNLP can be put to use in a variety of diverse corporate and individual environments, but it is most commonly used for healing, goal-setting, goal achievement, communication, motivation and team-building. By using ZeNLP techniques, managers will discover more about their employees in five minutes than they could previously do in two weeks. They will learn how to motivate their employees. More importantly, they will learn how their employees motivate themselves. ZeNLP teaches managers to create rapport and trust with prospective employees in a matter of minutes. It helps them to build motivation by creating opportunities that arise from this atmosphere of mutual trust and understanding. Advanced techniques like Mirroring and Anchoring help them to programme their employee's behaviour by targeting their unconscious minds!

How can managers benefit from ZeNLP? ZeNLP meditation techniques develop the fine art of aligning your energy in tune with the universal energy. This improves intuition, creativity and problem solving through right-brained thinking. ZeNLP mind power exercises push managers towards personal and organisational goals guided by the universal energy. ZeNLP meditation and music reduce stress levels of managers helping them to be calm while making crucial business decisions.

ZeNLP techniques are based on the new psychology of motivation. The process progresses as follows:

- Introduction
- Bond
- Trust
- Rapport
- Opportunity
- Motivation

ZeNLP is an entirely new system of motivation based on trust. People trust first, and then get motivated. If you can see Ram through his eyes, you will know how Ram gets motivated. All motivation is relationship motivation, personalised motivation or benefit motivation, but with ZeNLP you are pioneering insightful motivation. ZeNLP believes that people don't truly care how much you know until they know how much you care! Trust is created when the motivated and the motivator are in close physical, mental and spiritual rapport during the course of the interaction. Trust is created when managers use unconscious competence to motivate. Unconscious competence is communicating at an unconscious level.

ZeNLP researchers have discovered that people have three basic methods of perceiving the world based on our unconscious mental maps:

- Visual
- Auditory
- Kinesthetic

All of us have one of these preferred mental maps in our unconscious. The important point about these mental maps is that they are the preferred modes of thinking! A visual employee is most comfortable when you show him colourful brochures. It is his most natural way of understanding the world. An employee gets motivated faster when you can communicate with him in his preferred mode.

Former Indian cricket player Sunil Gavaskar is the classical example of a visual. Gavaskar could spot the ball faster and could visualise the ball's speed and trajectory accurately and, hence, went on to become the world's leading scorer of runs in test cricket. Any movement behind the sightscreen used to unnerve Gavaskar and many of his dismissals were a direct result of movement of spectators behind the bowler's arm. Being a visual, a slight movement near the sightscreen could distract the little master.

Wicket-keeper Sadanand Vishwanath is the classic example of an auditory. The victory of the Indian team at the World Series Cup in Australia, was a direct result of the motivation provided by the vociferous Sadanand. His spectacular stumpings and catches were a direct result of his ears picking up the faint sound of the ball on bat. Sadanand could predict the movement of the ball based on the type of sound made. He could make out the faint differences between the sound of the ball hitting the bat, pad or pitch and could effectively convert half chances into wickets. He always dived in the right direction at the right time, directed by his auditory abilities. This resulted in him effecting more dismissals behind the wickets, while conceding few byes and leg-byes.

Gundappa Vishwanath, the other little master, is the classic example of a kinesthetic. Vishwanath was a wristy player who waved his bat like a magic wand and the ball flew to the boundary! His elegant square cuts were a direct result of his fine sense of touch.

ZeNLP researchers believe that each one of us is either a Gavaskar, Sadanand or Vishwanath based on our preferred mental map. In India, 35 per cent of us are visuals, 35 per cent are auditories, and the rest of us are kinesthetics. This is a rough estimate based on an Internet based research study carried out between 1997 to 2004 at our website: http://www.tips4ceos.com/ research.htm This ZeNLP questionnaire was emailed to 10,000 email addresses out of which 1000 responses were received which were analysed. Another such study conducted independently by collecting printed questionnaires distributed to 3000 respondents scattered all over India confirmed the results of the email survey.

These ratios differ from country to country and sales presentations can be amended based on these differences. These statistics can dictate strategies of export-oriented corporates. For example, the French are predominantly auditories, the Russians are predominantly kinesthetics while the South Africans are predominantly visuals. ZeNLP techniques help to build trust. Once trust is built, motivation will follow. While motivating visuals, unconscious trust can be created by using visual predicates in your motivation talk. Predicates are words that reflect the unconscious mind. 'I *see* what you say', 'We have *colourful* paintings in each of our rooms'; 'Our hotel offers a panoramic *view* of the city,' etc. In the preceding statements, the words 'see', 'colourful' and 'view' are visual predicates. Similarly, *hear* is a auditory predicate, while *feel* is a kinesthetic predicate. When you communicate to your employees in their own mode they will get motivated faster.

ZeNLP techniques to build trust include Auto-suggestion, Movie Music, Ring of Excellence, Listening, Creative Visualisation, Meditation, Empathising, Mirroring, Anchoring, Stealing Anchors, Paraphrase listening, Pacing, Metaphors, Zen stories and Reframing. Thus, ZeNLP can be used to programme your employees to get motivated faster. It is all a matter of using the appropriate programming technique to elicit the desired outcome. The mind is the laboratory where ZeNLP experiments are carried out. Upgrading your software is as easy as changing your thoughts, in the way the brain codes experiences. ZeNLP shows you this way.

The benefits of ZeNLP for managers, entrepreneurs, professionals and public service officers can be summarised as follows:

- ZeNLP teaches managers the importance of goal setting in personal as well as professional life through the medium of stories. ZeNLP techniques help managers reach these goals through a combination of meditation, mind power exercises and positive affirmations. Managers can use the techniques discussed in this book for faster career growth and promotions which will directly contribute to organisational growth.

- Effective stress management through Zen meditation will increase the efficiency of managers who practise ZeNLP meditations described in this book. Managers who follow ZeNLP diet will benefit from lower cholesterol levels, higher immunity, increased anti-oxidants and lesser number of free radicles thus lowering healthcare-related expenses, leading to cost savings and increased profitability for their organisations. Tree plantation meditation inculcates environment consciousness among managers leading to enhanced self image and a sense of social responsibility. Clapping meditation leads to harmony in family life and reduces conflicts between family and career goals. These benefits can be multiplied manifold down the line, enabling organisations to adapt to the dynamically changing environment due to globalisation.

This book attempts to improve the SQ (Spiritual Quotient) score of managers. Managers with higher SQ scores are right-brain thinkers. This makes them more effective and efficient in managerial decision-making. ZeNLP cultivates right brain activity through meditation, creative visualisation and auto-suggestion.

A great Samurai warlord came to the Zen master and asked: 'Is there really paradise and a hell?' 'Who are you?' enquired the master. 'I am a Samurai,' the soldier replied. 'You a soldier!' exclaimed the master. 'What kind of ruler will have you as a guard? Your face looks like a beggar.' The Samurai became so angry that he began to draw his sword, but the Zen master continued: 'So you have a sword! Your weapon is too dull to cut off my head.' As the Samurai drew his sword, the master remarked: 'Here open the gates of hell!' At these words the Samurai, perceiving the master's discipline, sheathed his sword and bowed. 'Here open the gates of paradise,' said the Zen master. ZeNLP techniques can enrich your personal and professional life. The 'answer' is in your hands.

chapter 3
metaphors in ZeNLP!

ZeNLP is commonly called the 'Operating manual for the brain'. It is a practical yet comprehensive set of tools that can assist you in knowing and achieving excellence in your own field.

- Zen came from *dhyan* which means meditation.
- Neuro refers to our neurology. Our neurological connections are likened to roadways within our mind and re-occurring habits are just worn-out ruts of the mind. Our thoughts travel along these roadways, usually automatically. Expanding your choices of roads to travel is easy and simply starts with awareness of your thoughts. (*Zen Meditation*)
- Linguistic refers to your language. Language is a symbol that shapes our inner and outer experience.

When used with awareness, language can expand your view and experience of life. (*Auto-suggestion*)

- Programming refers to our deeply-conditioned thought patterns or programmes. Programmes or beliefs are accepted continuously, usually without awareness and simply run themselves on automatic pilot. Your deep underlying beliefs are always actualised in the outer world. Becoming aware of the programmes that run you can in itself be enough to create change, and also bring freedom and choice. (*Creative Visualisation*)

It is no 'meaningful coincidence' that since Vedic times, Indian rishis have been meditating, chanting powerful mantras and creatively visualising through epics like the Mahabharata and the Ramayana. More importantly, stories have played a major role in establishing new neural pathways in our brains and moulding the psyche of Indian children over generations. India has a rich tradition of 'teaching' stories, be it the *Jataka* tales, *Panchatantra* or the numerous other legendary tales which were vividly pictured in *Amar Chitra Katha*. Many of our legendary stories were exported to other Far East countries and continue to flourish in countries like Indonesia and Malaysia. With the spread of Buddhism, our '*Jataka* tales' took on a Japanese hue and appear in their Japanese *avtar* as Zen stories.

Today, Fortune 500 corporations have rephrased Zen stories as CMT (Corporate Myth Training) and have generated legendary experiences from which corporate myths grow. These legendary experiences are woven into ZeNLP training programmes and are an intricate part of creating new neural pathways in the brain. ZeNLP phrases this technique as 'metaphor'. Metaphors increase the efficiency and effectiveness of any training programme as they simplify ideas, are easy to recall and touch the emotions. ZeNLP is a system of training by which Zen stories are intricately woven into corporate training programmes, increasing effectiveness by appealing to the participants and driving the point into unconscious minds of trainees. Our grandma's tales are the hottest new weapons in the training armoury of Fortune 500 multinationals. The best thing about ZeNLP is that far-reaching changes can be brought about in attitudes, through the language of stories. Moreover, these changes are permanent—the dream of every corporate trainer.

An elderly woman walks into a store and tells the employee behind the counter that the tyres just aren't up to her standards, they haven't performed well and she really needs her money back. 'Are you sure you purchased them from here?' the employee asks. 'Quite sure,' replies the woman. 'I know I bought these tyres right here'. But the store does not sell tyres. With a bit of quick checking, the employee learns from his manager that the store which is just a few years old, had been built on the site of an old petrol pump— which likely sold the woman her tyres. So the employee takes

Rs 500 from the register, gives it to the woman, and apologises about the tyres not meeting her expectations. He asks her if there is anything else he can do for her, and when she declines, he sends her on her way with a smile.

We creatively visualised this powerful story and used it to maximum effect while training a group of fresh management graduates who had joined customer services at a department store chain. Stories can be creatively visualised by making them create an impact even though the story may be factually untrue. The creativity part comes in when you invent a fictional story on the spot! However, it is the impact of the story that is important in ZeNLP! Dr Milton H. Erickson, one of the world's leading hypnotherapists, could put patients into a profound trance, just by telling them stories.

Disney employees are trained to create what they term as 'magic moments' for their guests. Here is a story of how one Disney worker who did just that.

A Disney employee noticed two women at one of their theme parks, one posing for a picture, the other preparing to shoot it. The Disney employee walked up to the pair and offered to take a shot of both of them. The women happily agreed. A few months later the employee received a letter through his supervisor. It was from one of the women in the picture. As it turned out the women were sisters who hadn't spoken to each other in years. Their family, knowing the sisters were tired of their self-proclaimed feud, pitched

*in and sent them to 'the happiest place on earth' to become
reacquainted and set aside their differences. The women
had a wonderful time at Disney and the experience marked
a new beginning for their relationship. Shortly after the
visit, however, one sister became ill and died. The photograph taken by the Disney employee was the only one of the
two sisters on their special reconciliation trip. It meant the
world to the surviving sister and she wrote to Disney to
express her appreciation.* Not all Disney stories are quite
so touching.

Or, take the story of the little girl who was visiting
her aunt, a Disney employee, at the Magic Kingdom.
The girl desperately wanted to meet Snow White. At
the end of the day, the younger visitor had done
everything and seen everyone except Snow White. The
girl was heartbroken. So her aunt decided to break a
company rule and take the child a few steps behind the
scenes to find Snow White backstage. Sure enough,
there was Snow White—drinking a cup of coffee and
smoking a cigarette. This story jolts Disney employees
and they are more likely to remember the rules: For
employees—Never take visitors backstage. For actors
and actresses—Never ever depart from your character
while in costume. The best part about training through
stories is that the mental software is upgraded perma-
nently and these beliefs are actualised in the outer world
leading to no breakage of rules by all employees who
attend ZeNLP-based training.

One day there was an earthquake that shook the entire Zen temple. Parts of it even collapsed. Many of the monks were terrified. When the earthquake stopped, the teacher said, 'Now you have had the opportunity to see how a Zen man behaves in a crisis. You may have noticed that I did not panic. I was quite aware of what was happening and what to do. I led you all to the kitchen, the strongest part of the temple. It was a good decision because, you see, we have all survived without any injuries. However, despite my self-control and composure, I did feel a little tense—which you may have deduced from the fact that I drank a large glass of water, something I never do under ordinary circumstances. One of the monks smiled, but didn't say anything. 'What are you laughing about?' asked the teacher. 'That wasn't water,' the monk replied. 'It was a large glass of soya sauce.'

This book is full of metaphors. The objective of including small, thought-provoking anecdotes from Zen philosophy is two-fold. The first objective is to slide the reader into the main article by keeping his interest alive. Secondly, metaphors help to create an emotional bond with the readers and evoke their thinking process.

A university professor went to visit a famous Zen master. While the master quietly served tea, the professor talked about Zen. The master poured the visitor's cup to the brim, and then kept on pouring. The professor watched the overflowing cup until he could no longer restrain himself. 'It's overfull! No more will go in!' the professor blurted out. 'You are like this cup,' the master replied. 'How can I show you Zen unless you first empty your cup?'

There is a great truth hidden behind this simple Zen story. We can learn more from ancient wisdom than all modern researchers put together. Modern research has ignored ancient wisdom for long. The ZeNLP classifications of visual, auditory and kinesthetic based on our unconscious maps have been elucidated in great detail in the Chandogya Upanishad. Ancient Greek, Egyptian, Mayan and Biblical manuscripts also talk about the importance of the elements (fire, water and earth) and the dominance of one element over the others.

In ancient times it was known that all the myriad things were created from the essence of five elements: Water, air, earth, fire, and ether. They endowed the cosmos with substance, and gave their spirit to all that had life. But over the ages the races grew proud and separated the five elements from spirit, spirit from virtue and virtue from self. Now the knowledge of the prime elements is all but lost; spirit and virtue have been lost with it. The five elements were condensed into three as air came from fire and sky from earth.

The Universe, according to ancient Indian thinking, is composed of five basic elements, the *Pancha Mahabootas*: *Prithivi* (earth), *Apya* (water), *Teja* (fire), *Vayu* (air) and *Akash* (ether). As the human body is similarly constituted, there is a fundamental harmony between the universe and man, a healthy balance between the microcosm and macrocosm.

Ayurveda is the theory of *Tridosha*: *Vata*, *Pitta* and *Kapha*. *Vata* is a combination of two elements of the universe—air and ether, *Pitta* an amalgam of fire and earth and *Kapha* the combination of ether and water. According to this theory, the *Tridoshas*, remain in a balanced state in the human body and, when this balance is disturbed, it results in disease. In Zen philosophy, the red square represents fire, the blue triangle represents water and the green circle represents earth. According to Zen, these fundamental shapes symbolise the three primordial elements. At a deeper level, they represent the body, mind and soul.

Ancient Chinese philosophy also lists the five elements as fire, water, earth, wood and metal. Thus, the elements common to the Indian *Pancha Mahabhootas* and Chinese are fire, water and earth.

Egyptian scriptures say that all substances are composed of some combination of the three elements: earth, fire, and water. A time-tested way of finding out what things are made of is 'Analysis by fire'. When you heat a substance, it releases its constituent elements. For example, when you heat a metal, it is transformed into fire and calyx (a form of earth).

Metal → fire + calyx (earth)

This shows that metals are made up of the elements earth and fire.

When glucose is combusted in the human body to liberate energy, it is transformed into some energy and heat (fire), and a lot of water, and some earth.

Glucose → water + fire + earth (water + energy + urea)

Some substances, like coal or wax, contain so much fire that once you get them started, the fire continues to escape on its own, and little may be left but earth (ashes from burning coal). In the case of wax, almost nothing is left, indicating it was made of almost pure fire (plus a little water and earth). Thus, we can analyse any substance and determine the combination of the three elements that make it up.

Similarly, all human beings are also made up of a combination of these three elements, but one of these three elements dominates the other two, classifying humanity into three distinct energy bodies based on the dominance of fire, water or earth.

The qualities associated with each element are:

- Water: peaceful, compassionate/deep, fluid/turbulent, relentless
- Earth: supportive, reliable/calculating, steadfast/crushing, tumultuous
- Fire: warm, comforting/quick-tempered, courageous/swift destruction, chaotic

The Greek philosopher Empedocles classified the elements as earth, fire and water in the 5th century BC.

He was following the Pythagorean philosophies, which divided the world into four elements, four seasons, and four stages of life. He taught that the human being is composed as the world is. The Greeks extensively discussed the origins of life. This marks the beginning of their philosophy. This notion was then developed into the ideas of hot, cold, moist and dry that made up Hippocrates' four humours.

The belief that there are five elements is universal. In China, for example, the elements are: earth, fire, water, wood, and metal. The fifth element arises from the union of the other four. The notion of five elements is particular to the Western tradition and, curiously, it is shared by the Indian one. Did they all originate from a common source and was the theory passed on to the West (or the other way), or did they fall under the notion of 'independent evolution'? Or, did they all connect to cosmic consciousness far early in their evolution?

In the myths about the creation of the world, one element is usually thought to have existed before the others. Most stories about creation recount that in the beginning everything was covered with water. The earth appeared afterwards, either out of the water, or by being put upon the water. Of course, creation myths vary from culture to culture, and each one is more fantastic than the other.

The Book of Genesis in The Bible says:

Out of Fire came Water
Out of Fire and Water came Earth.

There is a Rig Vedic hymn which says...

Earth, who of yore was Water in the oceans.

Within Christianity, for example, many might remember how Moses met his God, as a burning bush, and the Holy Spirit is also represented as a flame. The same element, though, has been used to symbolise what is considered evil—passion is related to flames. This tradition was widely used in Renaissance allegories, where the flames of passion surround Lust, one of the seven deadly sins.

In China, fire (*huo*) is masculine (*yang*) and generally has positive symbolism: wrath, danger, speed, and lust. Fire is also purification. In ancient times, corpses of those who died because of contagious illnesses were burned. Cities were burned down to eradicate them. Fire is powerful and fascinates us humans. It has helped our lives since the beginning, allowing for the growth of technology, making our life easier. The first caveman who tasted a piece of meat that had fallen into the fire must have been very happy indeed! And from there on we have applied it to our daily life.

In astrology and palmistry (just because I know there are a lot of people out there interested in it—too many, if you ask an expert palmist like me), fire is related to a physical personality. Water is the primordial element from which all was created, at least according to many creation myths. It is an archaic symbol of the womb and of fertility; also of purification and rebirth. The image of the earth rising from the water (widespread in many early civilizations) gives it its womb-like connotations, thus relating it to motherhood. The zodiac signs too are divided into water, earth and fire signs. Watering plants to make them grow symbolises the nourishment of the intellect.

Empedocles was one of the first philosophers to put forth a theory based on all three elements—earth water and fire—rather than just one. He said that matter consisted of all three elements, but in various quantities (a stone had more earth while the sea had more water). He also believed there were two forces—love and hate, or eros and strife—which cause the elements to come together or move apart.

'Nature's Laws are the invisible government of the earth,' said Alfred A. Montapert. This is one of the great truths and all knowledge emanates from *Prakriti* (Cosmic Nature). Similarly, the ZeNLP classification of humans into visuals, auditories and kinesthetics is given in the Vedas. Individuals in whom the element of fire dominates over water and earth are visuals; water dominates in auditories and earth in kinesthetics. ZeNLP meditation includes identifying the element dominating the individual and connecting to it to liberate large amounts of cosmic energy which helps attain inner peace.

One day, the sun and the wind were having a discussion about who was more powerful than the other. They noticed a tired traveller wearing a huge overcoat trudging through a desert. They decided that whoever could make the traveller remove his overcoat first was more powerful. The wind tried first. It started blowing against the traveller. The more fiercely the wind blew, the tighter the traveller held on to his coat. After a lot of effort wind gave up. Then the sun tried. It shone on the traveller, till he started to sweat. The sun increased its intensity and soon the traveller became so uncomfortably hot that he removed his overcoat. Persuasion can win, when brute force fails.

chapter 4
how ZeNLP works?

ZeNLP techniques such as creative visualisation, auto-suggestion and relaxation meditation can be used by managers to enhance their personal effectiveness and team effectiveness. Managers who start practising these exercises soon find themselves being guided by their inner intelligence and these exercises seamlessly fit into your daily routine almost without any special effort.

As ZeNLP exercises employ the power of the unconscious mind, maximum results can be obtained with minimum effort, as exemplified by this Zen story.

Roshi Chapel agreed to educate a group of psychoanalysts about Zen. After being introduced to the group by the director of the analytic institute, Roshi quietly sat on a cushion placed on the floor. A student entered, prostrated before the master, and then seated himself on another cushion a few feet away, facing his teacher. 'What is Zen?' the student asked. Roshi produced a banana, peeled it, and started eating. 'Is that all? Can't you show me anything else?' the student said. 'Come closer, please,' the master replied. The student moved in and Roshi waved the remaining portion of the banana before the student's face. The student prostrated, and left. A second student rose to address the audience. 'Do you all understand?' When there was no response, the student added, 'You have just witnessed a first-rate demonstration of Zen. Are there any questions?' After a long silence, someone spoke up. 'Roshi, I am not satisfied with your demonstration. You have shown us something that I am not sure I understand. It must be possible to tell us what Zen is.' 'If you must insist on words,' the Roshi replied, 'then Zen is an elephant copulating with a flea'.

To many this may seem contradictory but therein lies the catch. Zen is a form of meditation which has to be experienced to understand the power. It is as delicate as when an elephant prepares to make love to a flea. Is that possible? Yes, it is. The mind needs to discipline itself to the extent an elephant must discipline itself before making love to a flea.

ZeNLP exercises employ the fine art of unconscious competence, or the ability to generate results without making a conscious effort. All you need to do is programme your unconscious mind through creative visualisation, auto-suggestion and meditation. Soon, one will be led to events and coincidences which propel one towards a goal. One always reaches the right place at the right time and makes the right choices to reach the goal, smarter and faster.

A Zen master asked his disciple to bring him a pail of water to cool his bath. The student brought the water and, after cooling the bath, poured to the ground the remaining water. 'You dunce!' the master scolded him. 'Why din't you give the rest of the water to the trees?'

This book is an experiential guide that will lead you to the water; but you have to drink. One has to plant a sapling (goal)in a fertile ground (mind). But that is not enough. One has to nurture the sapling through regularly watering it. In other words, one has to practise the ZeNLP mind power exercises on a daily basis to get results. The answer lies in your hands.

chapter 5

creative visualisation in ZeNLP

Creative visualisation, day-dreaming or imagination, call it what you will but there is a great truth in the saying *As he thinketh in his mind so is he*. Whatever the mind conceives and believes, it achieves. The first step towards goal achievement always starts with visualisation, creative visualisation. It always begins with a mental idea, an image. Thoughts are powerful and relaxation meditation followed by creative visualisation generates powerful results in a short period of time.

ZeNLP combines meditation with NLP mind power exercises to generate powerful results in the shortest possible time frame. The visualisation exercises are goal specific but the techniques remain the same. Managers must set their short, medium and long-term goals over a period of five, 10 and 20 years down the line. Goals must be put down in writing and have to be specific, measurable, ambitious, realistic and achieved within a specified time frame. These goals have to be written and memorised till they sink into the unconscious.

Regular sessions of meditation and creative visualisation are needed to constantly programme the mind to reach towards these objectives. Progress towards these goals are measured by analysing dream diaries. Recording of dreams is the most important aspect of ZeNLP as dream analysis provides various clues about progress. Similarly, dreams also provide an indication of deviations from goals, if any, so that corrective measures can be incorporated into the daily activities.

Case study 1

V.G. is a 36-year-old trainer who set his long-term goal to successfully expand his training activities to the US. He wanted to be successful financially and dreamt of international recognition. He wanted to conduct cutting-edge personal effectiveness and team effectiveness training programmes for Fortune 500 companies.

V.G. was recommended to mentally visualise the following exercises, once, if not twice a day, after relaxation meditation.

Exercise 1

He is being flown in a corporate helicopter from the rooftop of a Manhattan skyscraper to the rooftop of a convention centre hosting his training programme. Soon, he has a bird's eye view of Manhattan. As he sees the convention centre, he visualises, the participants waiting at the rooftop, awaiting his arrival. He is asked to click an aerial photograph of the convention centre's roof as seen from the helicopter. Then he is asked to freeze a frame, like a still picture from a movie, which symbolises the event. The picture should be bright and in colour.

Next, he frames this picture in a golden picture frame, and hangs it in his mind. He is asked to visit this framed photograph in his mental picture gallery daily during his visits to the tree planted by him, based on his mental map or date of birth. Regular visits to the tree, and creatively visualising the framed picture of his goal, starts a chain reaction which propel him towards the goal based on a series of meaningful coincidences.

V.G.'s mental map was kinesthetic, so he was asked to plant a neem sapling in front of his residence and water it daily while going for his morning walk. He had to water the tree three times, saying 'OM' thrice, barefoot, after sunrise and creatively visualising the helicopter exercise by closing his eyes. V.G. was also asked to maintain a detailed diary of his dreams from day one. He had to follow a vegan diet, on the days he visited the tree. The days he deviated from the diet, he could do the creative visualisation exercises when he drove to the office. To keep track of the growth of the sapling, he was asked to photogaph the tree on the first day of every year.

As the sapling is watered daily, it begins to sprout new leaves, and starts growing! At the same time, meaningful coincidences are created which help participants to reach their goal, by harnessing the infinite power of cosmic consiousness within oneself. It is no coincidence that a tree needs the right combination of sunlight, water and earth for its optimal growth. Unless and until, all the events in the universe are synchronised by cosmic consciousness, so that the right events happen at the right time, goals cannot be reached. Visiting the tree, while being in touch with the primordial cosmic elements of fire, water and earth and creatively visualising the goal achievement exercises, energises your unconscious mind, and the infinite intelligence within you begins to guide you moment by moment towards your destination. The biggest advantage of ZeNLP is that it works on the principle of obtaining maximum results through minimum effort. ZeNLP guides you to harness the power of cosmic consciousness resident within you to create the right coincidences at the right time to propel you towards your personal, organisational, health and financial goals. At the time of writing, V.G. is slowly but surely on his way to his goal as he has successfully completed five years of creative visualisation and his sapling is growing well.

Case study 2

R.C., 44, is the DGM of a large public sector organisation, heading the most profitable division of this mega-corporation. During our ZeNLP workshop, R.C. set his 10 year goal to become the CMD of his own company. R.C. planted an Ashoka tree and nurtured it carefully over two years. At the same time, he practised the following creative visualisations at his tree every day.

Exercise 1

R.C. was told to visualise himself 10 years into the future as CMD of RC Industries Pvt. Ltd. He was told to see himself being chauffeur driven into a factory. He walks into the factory and takes the lift to his cabin. Outside his cabin, he was told to see a gleaming brass board proclaiming "R.C. CMD, RC Industries Pvt. Ltd. He was asked to mentally click the photograph of this shining and bold nameplate. R.C. then had to frame this picture in a golden picture frame, and hang it in the picture gallery of his mind. He was asked to visit this framed photograph in his mental picture gallery as often as he could.

Exercise 2

R.C. was given powerful auto-suggestions for repetition like a mantra. These 10 auto-suggestions when repeated in a step-by-step method, thrice daily while listening to special mind power music based on his mental map. As R.C. was an auditory, he had to read these auto-suggestions while playing water music. Water music is music of the mountain streams, seas and flowing water, set to instruments like the flute, santoor and jaltarang. He did this so that the auto-suggestion could sink into his unconscious mind faster, before leaving for office or on the way to the office, while in the back seat of his car.

R.C. had to first play the water music, read the auto-suggestions for success, aloud, once. He had to repeat this exercise, without the music, while he was seated in his cabin, after the lunch break. R.C. had to repeat the morning's exercise, after dinner. Alternatively, he could do it in the back seat of his car if he was getting delayed in the office. He was requested to carry the water cassette and a Walkman, on all his outstation trips, so that his ZeNLP exercises would not be missed even for a day. CD-ROMs and MP3 files with fire, water and earth music is available online at our website tips4ceos.com to enable participants to complete their exercises throughout the world. While water music is for auditories, fire is for visuals and earth for kinesthetics.

R.C. was asked to follow a strict vegan diet while visiting the tree and while reading these auto-suggestions for success. He was also asked to maintain a detailed, dated dream diary of all dreams seen since he started his ZeNLP exercises. These dream diaries were to be emailed once a month to evaluate his progress towards his goals.

At the time of writing, R.C. is slowly but surely on his way to his goal as he has successfully completed three years of creative visualisation and his sapling is growing well. At present, R.C. has successfully emailed dream diaries for the seventh auto-suggestion for success and is continuing with the eighth.

chapter 6

the vedic connection of ZeNLP

Every 10 years, the monks were permitted to speak just two words. After spending his first 10 years at the monastery, one monk went to the head monk. 'It has been 10 years,' said the head monk. 'What are the two words you would like to speak?' 'Bed... hard...' said the monk. 'I see,' replied the head monk. Ten years later, the monk returned to the head monk's office. 'It has been 10 more years,' said the head monk. 'What are the two words you would like to speak?' 'Food... stinks...,' said the monk. 'I see,' replied the head monk. Yet another 10 years passed and the monk once again met the head monk who asked, 'What are your two words now, after these 10 years?' 'I... quit!' said the monk. 'Well, I can see why,' replied the head monk. 'All you ever do is complain.'

There is a great truth hidden behind this simple Zen story. Our neural pathways are roads by which our thoughts travel unconsciously. ZeNLP techniques develop the fine art of becoming competent without becoming conscious. This is known as unconscious competence and this skill can be honed by programming our hardware (brain) with the appropriate software. The human brain can be programmed by sight, sound, taste, smell and touch or a combination of these senses. ZeNLP works by analysing your preferred mental map. The analysis of the preferred mental map is the most important part of ZeNLP and the classification of individuals into visual, auditory and kinesthetic is integral to the success of ZeNLP. Interestingly, ZeNLP techniques are being used by a majority of us who are religious. Consider Islam, where at a particular time all Muslims have to face the East and look towards the *Kabah*. That is visual. Then comes the auditory part of the *azaan*, or the call of the *mullah*, and during prayer all of them touch the ground (kinesthetic). All the three vital factors of ZeNLP—the visual, the auditory and the kinesthetic—are involved. The scientific concept behind this is that when millions gather and bow down and touch the ground in prayer, it liberates a tremendous amount of cosmic energy. That is one of the reasons for the strong bonding between the followers of Islam.

The Vedas also talk about *prakriti* (cosmic nature). Cosmic nature, mother of all vibrations, has three phases: the creative, preservative and dissolving states and these three modes of Nature appear as the Creator or Brahma (*rajas*), the Preserver or Vishnu (*sattva*) and the destroyer or Shiva (*tamas*). An analysis of the Rig Vedic code reveals that each of these states of cosmic nature are present in humans but one of these states dominates the other two. Thus, individuals in whom *sattva* dominates are visuals, *rajas* dominates are auditories and *tamas* dominates are kinesthetics. Activities that involve all the three states attract visuals, auditories and kinesthetics, liberate cosmic energy and programmes all of them to return and re-experience the magic. Going to a temple also touches all the three categories exemplified by ringing the temple bell (auditories), *aarti* (visual) and *namaskar* (kinesthetic).

Our research has shown that going to a beach, tree plantations, meditation and yoga are activities which connect one to the cosmic energy. At the beach, the roaring water attracts auditories, the setting sun attracts the visuals and the moist sand attracts the kinesthetics. Hence each ZeNLP personality is linked to an element. Auditories to water (*varuna*), visuals to sun (*surya*) and kinesthetics to earth (*bhoomi*). One of these elements dominates the other two. The objective of ZeNLP meditation is to move away from being single-sensory human beings to evolve into multi-sensory human beings. The Rig Veda states that Gods of the cosmos reside inside our brains, which is a metaphor signifying the presence of Brahma, Vishnu and Shiva in our unconscious minds. ZeNLP works on three kinds of programming, depending on the predominant trait of an individual—visual, auditory or kinesthetic (touch). This trait is determined by the dominance of one of the Gods over the others and the dominance of one type of element over the others.

The Vedas say: *Prakriti* means a special (*pra*) creation (*kriti*) of Mayadevi for the sole purpose of material creation. *Prakriti* also means that which creates. It has three *Gunas*, and *gnaan* (knowledge) *shakti*, *kriyaa* (action) *shakti*, and *tattv shakti* or material energy. The combination of three Gunas of *prakriti* is called *mahat tattv*, *mahat brahm*, or cosmic mind. *Mahat tattv* is called cosmic mind, because it creates. The cosmic mind when acted upon by *Niraakaar Dev* produces *ahamkaar tattv*. If *Prakriti* is the milk, *niraakaar* is the process that produces ghee of ahamkaar from the cream of *mahat*. *Taamasik ahamkaar* produces five elements and corresponding five senses (or *tanmaatraas*) (earth-touch, water-hearing, fire-sight, air-smell, and ether-taste).

Ancient Indian ayurveds analysed the element dominant in the patient before commencing any treatment. Ayurveda classifies humans into *vaat*, *pith* and *kaph* based on the element dominating the mind. They had the knowledge that visual patients responded best to colour therapy, auditories to music or raaga therapy, and kinesthetics to reiki and pranic healing. Thus, ancient Indian rishis asked auditories to chant powerful mantras, while visuals were told to mentally visualise colours and kinesthetics were given yogic exercises and asked to meditate using *rudraksh malas*. The classification of individuals was so perfect that Lord Krishna who was an incarnation of Vishnu has been described as a visual, whereas Arjuna has been classified as an auditory. Thus, Lord Krishna recited the Bhagavad Geeta to Arjuna.

A martial arts student approached his teacher with a question. 'I'd like to improve my knowledge of the martial arts. In addition to learning from you, I'd like to study with another teacher in order to learn another style. What do you think of this idea?' 'The hunter who chases two rabbits,' answered the master, 'catches neither.'

Just as this Zen story which was written thousands of years before Henri Fayol propounded the same story as a principle of management phrased by him as Unity of Command (every subordinate should report to one boss). All major religions and the Vedas have built ZeNLP techniques into their prayers, rituals and rites ensuring our minds will be programmed correctly if we follow our holy books ensuring that all religious traditions will endure and last as long as our universe exists.

chapter 7
the power of ZeNLP
mantras

Two travelling monks reached a river where they met a young woman. Wary of the current, she asked if they could carry her across. One of the monks hesitated, but the other quickly picked her up onto his shoulders, transported her across the water, and put her down on the other bank. She thanked him and departed. As the monks continued on their way, one was brooding and preoccupied. Unable to hold his silence, he spoke out. 'Brother, our spiritual training teaches us to avoid any contact with women, but you picked that one up on your shoulders and carried her!' 'Brother,' the second monk replied, 'I set her down on the other side, while you are still carrying her.'

There is a great truth behind this simple Zen story. Most of us carry a lot of excess baggage in our minds. Negative memories which we continue to carry in our mental hardware have to be deleted or sent to the trash can. ZeNLP meditation is one way by which such negative memories are transferred to the trash can. Just as simple stories, parables and epics can programme the mind of children, similarly chanting of mantras like *Namyaho Renge Kyo*, *Om Mani Padme Hum*, in relaxed surroundings can programme stress out of our mind.

A saying from the Vedas claims that *Speech is the essence of humanity*. All of what humanity thinks and ultimately becomes is determined by the expression of ideas and actions through speech and its derivative— writing. Everything, the Vedas maintain, comes into being through speech. Ideas remain unactualised until they are created through the power of speech. Similarly, the Gospel of John in the New Testament starts, 'In the beginning was The Word. And the Word was with God and the Word was God...'

In mainstream Vedic practices, most Buddhist techniques and classical Hinduism, mantra is viewed as a necessity for spiritual advancement and high attainment. In *The Kalachakra Tantra*, by the Dalai Lama and Jeffrey Hopkins, the Dalai Lama states, 'Therefore, without depending upon mantra...Buddhahood cannot be attained.'

Clearly, there is a reason why such widely divergent sources of religious wisdom as the vedas, the New

Testament and the Dalai Lama speak in common ideas. Here are some important ideas about mantra which will enable you to gain a practical understanding of what mantra is and what it can do.

Mantras are energy-based sounds

Saying any word produces an actual physical vibration. Over time, if we know what the effect of that vibration is, then the word may come to have meaning associated with the effect of saying that vibration or word. This is one level of energy basis for words.

Another level is intent. If the actual physical vibration is coupled with mental intention, the vibration then contains an additional mental component which influences the result of saying it. Sound is the carrier wave and intent is overlaid upon the wave form, just as a coloured gel influences the appearance and effect of white light.

In either instance, the word is based upon energy. Nowhere is this idea truer than for Sanskrit mantras. Although there is a general meaning which is associated with mantras, the only lasting definition is the result or effect of saying the mantra.

Mantras create thought-energy waves

Human consciousness is a collection of states of consciousness which distributively exist throughout the physical and subtle bodies. Each organ has a primitive consciousness of its own that allows it to perform functions specific to it. Then come the various systems. The cardio-vascular system, the reproductive system and other systems have various organs or body parts working at slightly different stages of a single process. Like the organs, there is a primitive consciousness also associated with each system. These are just within the physical body. Similar functions and states of consciousness exist within the subtle body as well. So, individual organ consciousness is overlaid by system consciousness, overlaid again by subtle body counterparts and consciousness, and so ad infinitum.

The ego with its self-defined 'I'-ness assumes a pre-eminent state among the subtle din of random, unconscious thoughts which pulse through our organism. Of course, our organism can 'pick up' the vibrations from other organisms nearby. The result is that there are myriad vibrations riding in and through the unconscious mind at any given time. Mantras start a powerful vibration which corresponds to both a specific spiritual energy frequency and a state of consciousness in seed form. Over time, the mantra process begins to override all the other smaller vibrations, which eventually become absorbed by the mantra. After a length of time which varies from individual to individual, the great wave of the mantra stills all other vibrations. Ultimately, the mantra produces a state where the organism vibrates at the rate completely in tune with the energy and spiritual state represented by, and contained within, the mantra.

At this point, a change of state occurs in the organism. The organism becomes subtly different. Just as a laser is light which is coherent in a new way, the person who becomes one with the state produced by the mantra is also coherent in a way which did not exist prior to the conscious undertaking of repetition of the mantra.

Mantras are tools of power and tools for power

They are formidable. They are ancient. They work. The word 'mantra' is derived from two Sanskrit words. The first is *manas* or 'mind', which provides the 'man' syllable. The second syllable is drawn from the Sanskrit word *tra* meaning 'three'. Therefore, the word mantra in its most literal sense means 'three sounds that programme the mind.' Mantra is, at its core, a tool used by the mind which eventually frees one from the negative energies and negative memories of the mind.

But the journey from mantra to freedom is a wondrous one. The mind expands, deepens and widens and eventually dips into the essence of cosmic existence. On its journey, the mind comes to understand much about the essence of the vibration of things. Knowledge, as we all know, is power. In the case of mantra, this power is tangible and wieldable.

Mantras have close, approximate one-to-one direct language-based translation. If we warn a young child not to touch a hot stove, we try to explain that it will burn the child. However, language is insufficient to convey the experience. Only the act of touching the stove and being burned will adequately define the words 'hot' and 'burn' in the context of the 'stove'. Essentially, there is no real direct translation of the experience of being burned. Similarly, there is no word which is the exact equivalent of the experience of sticking one's finger into an electrical socket. When we stick our hand into the socket, only then do we have a context for the word 'shock'. But shock is really a definition of the result of the action of sticking our hand into the socket. It is the same with mantras. The only true definition is the experience which it ultimately creates in the sayer. Over thousands of years, many sayers have had common experiences and passed them on to the next generation. Through this tradition, a context of experiential definition has been created.

The power of the maha mantra Om has been explained as follows in the Upanishads:

> *Chandogya Upanishad says...*
> *Earth is the essence of Life*
> *Water is the essence of Earth*
> *Herbs are the essence of Water*
> *Man is the essence of Herbs*
> *Speech is the essence of Man*

Vedas are the essence of Speech
OM is the essence of the Vedas

Lord Krishna says in the Bhagavad Geeta, 'All meditation should begin with Om'. phenoMenon's ZeNLP
workshops include creative visualisation, auto-
suggestion, dynamic meditation and chanting of mantras to liberate cosmic energy.

A new student approached the Zen master and asked how
he should prepare himself for his training. 'Think of me as
a bell,' the master explained. 'Give me a soft tap, and you
will get a tiny ping. Strike hard, and you'll receive a loud,
resounding peal'.

chapter 8

the super power of Gayatri Mantra

There is a Zen story about a poor man walking through the woods reflecting upon his many troubles. He stopped to rest against a tree, a magical tree that would instantly grant the wishes of anyone who came in contact with it. He realised he was thirsty and wanted a drink. Instantly a cup of cool water was in his hand. Shocked, he looked at the water, he decided it was safe and drank it. He then realised he was hungry and wished he had something to eat. A meal appeared before him. 'My wishes are being granted,' he thought in disbelief. 'Well, then I wish for a beautiful home of my own,' he said out loud. The home appeared in the meadow before him. A huge smile crossed his face as he wished for servants to take care of the house. When they

*appeared he realised he had somehow been blessed with an
incredible power and he wished for a beautiful, loving,
intelligent woman to share his good fortune. 'Wait a minute,
this is ridiculous,' said the man to the woman. 'I'm not this
lucky. This can't happen to me.' As he spoke...everything
disappeared. He shook his head and said, 'I knew it,' then
walked away thinking about his many troubles.*

There is a great truth hidden behind this simple Zen
story. Our mind is like this magical tree. *Whatever the
mind conceives and believes, it achieves.* Since Vedic times,
this universal truth has been understood by our rishis.
Recitation of mantras is one of the tools for programming our unconscious minds. Alas, mantras are like the
magical tree mentioned in the Zen story narrated earlier.
Mantras work for those who believe in their power. The
Vedas, Upanishads and Samhitas are a rich source of
powerful mantras. Out of these mantras, the Gayatri
Mantra is known as the *Maha Mantra*. The Gayatri
Mantra has been recited over the ages by Indian rishis
and it has been accorded the pride of place among all
Vedic mantras. No lesser a Godhead than Sri Krishna
says in the Holy Geeta: '*Among Mantras I am Gayatri*'
The Vedika form of the famous Gayatri Mantra is:

*Om bhur-bhuvah-svah
tat savitur varenyam
bhargo devasya dhimahi
dhiyo yo nah pracodayat*

This can be translated: Om! Let us contemplate the spirit of the divine of the earth, the atmosphere and heaven. May that direct our minds. Savitur is the sun and this mantra is pronounced at the three junctions, or twilights, of the day.

The *tantrik* compilation *Prapanchasaratantra*, outlines pujas and meditations on Gayatri in great detail. Described here is how the mantra Om hums in the base or *Muladhara chakra*, and moves through seven stages to the chakra above the head. (*Sahasrara*).

According to our rishis, Mahavishnu describes Om as consisting of the following: *Bhuh* is existence, *Bhuva* is the elements, *Svah* is the *atma* of everything, *Maha* is greatness and light, *Tat* is Brahman (the absolute), *Tapah* is all knowledge, and *Satyam* is supremacy and internal wisdom. This *tantra* connects the three letters of Om (A+U+M) to the seven worlds. (See also *Jnanasankalini Tantra*.)

Tat refers to the first cause of all substance, as fire in the circle of the sun and is a supreme Brahman. *Savitur* is the source of all living beings. *Varenyam* is the excellent one who receives adoration. *Bharga* destroys sin, *Devasya* means it is full of light, while *Dhimahi* refers to knowledge being golden and always within the sun. *Dhiyo* means *Buddhi*, *Yo* stands for energy (*tejas*). The mantra is divided into three sections of eight letters and four sections of six letters. A *dhyana* (meditation) describes Gayatri as having three faces, which are white, red and black. (morning, afternoon, evening/visual, auditory, kinesthetic).

Yet, the tantrik tradition has newer views of the Gayatri. For example, in the *Matrikabhedatantra*, there is a couplet which says a person who knows the Brahman (the absolute), is a yogi. In the tantrik tradition, each aspect of *devata* has her or his own form of the Gayatri and it is often pronounced at the junctions of the day, including midnight.

For example, *Tripurasundari Gayatri* runs:

Tripurasundari vidmahe,
kameshvari dhimahi,
tanno klinne pracodayat.

This means: Let us contemplate Tripurasundari, let us think of Kameshvari, may that sweetness direct.

The *Gandharva Tantra* uses 24 different syllables of this mantra in Sanskrit as a visualisation, starting from the base of the spine and moving to the top of the head. The other tantrik Gayatri is a mantra known as *Ajapa*. This is recited by every living being unconsciously several hundred times a day as she or he breathes. Half are sun breaths and half are moon breaths. It consists of the letters *Ha* and *Sa*. In the morning, Gayatri takes the form of Brahma; in the afternoon of Vishnu and in the evening of Shiva. Thus, the recital of the Gayatri Mantra as per the ZeNLP classification of visuals, auditories and kinesthetics are given on the following page:

- Visuals—to recite in the morning followed by Chakra Meditation.
- Auditories—to recite in the afternoon followed by sound vibration.
- Kinesthetics—to recite in the evening followed by dynamic meditation.

This ZeNLP classification is on the basis of your preferred mental map. Thus, to derive maximum benefits from the recitation of the Gayatri Mantra, it is imperative to discover your preferred mental map and proceed with the recitation. The exact pronunciation of the Gayatri Mantra makes it necessary to begin this holy recitation under expert guidance. During ZeNLP workshops, this expert guidance is provided, based on the participant's preferred mental map.

The Gayatri Mantra has several variants, the primary among them being Agni Gayatri, Varuna Gayatri and Pruthvi Gayatri. Visuals are recommended to chant Agni Gayatri 108 times at dawn, Varuna Gayatri at noon and kinesthetics at dusk. Scientific chanting of these mantras awaken the cosmic consciousness faster.

God is the life of life, the light of the world, the eternal origin and support of the creative cycle of the universe. The sun is the metaphor of Divinity, being the generative support of life on earth. Vedas are the poetry of God uttered in meta-language, which is the sound correspondence of the Omniscience and infinite creative joy of Divinity, the power of Infinity, and the glory of immortality. In the Vedas, Savitur is a symbol of the Divine. On the plane of eternity, Savitur means God; on the physical plane, it means the sun; on the psychic plane it means intelligence; on the biological plane, it means vitality. The Gayatri Mantra (Yajur Veda, 36.3) is the essence of the Vedas.

Gayatri indeed is a quintessential reflection of the blazing omniscience of Divinity captured in 24 syllables. It is a homage to the sun the Sublime; a symbol of the radiance of the Divine vibrating through the earth, heaven, and the intervening spaces, inspiring life with energy, intelligence and blessed joy. The splendour of Lord Savitur, the Creator sun, is like the galactic explosion of a thousand suns bursting forth on the horizon in the first morning of the Universe—the same as Lord Krishna revealed to Arjuna in the Bhagavad Geeta.

The Gayatri Mantra moves us to superconscious elevation of the soul with the impact of its beauty, wonder and bliss. It consecrates us into a mood of prayer to participate in the creative ephiphany of the Universal Mother. It opens the floodgates of light and beatitude of peace and immortality to a world otherwise shaken by mortality and pain.

Managers can benefit by realising that mantras, *kalmas* and psalms are powerful auto-suggestion which programme the unconscious mind. As each manager has a special mode of programming his unconscious mind, these auto-suggestions can be made to sink into the unconscious faster, by identifying the preferred mental map and programming it appropriately. When powerful affirmations pertaining to personal and organisational goals sink into the unconscious, it enables managers to become unconsciously competent in achieving their goals. In other words, it increases their efficiency and effectiveness and enables them to achieve their goals through the path of least resistance. Unconscious competence enables managers to maximise results with minimum effort. In financial terms, this means minimising risks while maximising returns. In business language, unconscious competence ensures maximum profit at minimum cost. In spiritual terms, unconscious competence means harnessing the power of the infinite intelligence within you to achieve your goals.

A martial arts student went to his teacher and said earnestly, 'I am devoted to studying your martial system. How long will it take me to master it.' The teacher's reply was casual, '10 years' Impatiently, the student answered, 'But I want to master it faster than that. I will work very hard. I will practise everyday, 10 or more hours a day if I have to. How long will it take then?' The teacher thought for a moment, '20 years.'

chapter 9
programming the human mind

A renowned Zen master said his greatest teaching was this: Buddha is your own mind. So impressed by how profound this idea was, one monk decided to leave the monastery and retreat to the wilderness to meditate on this insight. There he spent 20 years as a hermit probing the great teaching. One day he met another monk who was travelling through the forest. Quickly, the hermit monk learned that the traveller also had studied under the same Zen master. 'Please, tell me what you know of the master's greatest teaching.' The traveller's eyes lit up, 'Ah, the master has been very clear about this. He says that his greatest teaching is this: Buddha is your own mind.'

It has been estimated by neuro-surgeons that human beings utilise only a fraction of the immense potential of the brain. There are two billion neurons in the brain. Imagine two billion Pentium chips. They represent two billion stand alone PCs. Powerful, yes but the power is finite as these PCs cannot talk to each other. Now, interconnect these PCs through high-speed optic fibre cables. Each of these two billion PCs are connected to each other in every possible way. Now calculate the power of this two billion PC network. The processing power of each PC increases exponentially with the addition of each PC to the network. What do we get?

We get an Internet which is a billion times powerful than the one that exists today! This is a simple metaphor to illustrate the power of the human brain. Each one of us is empowered with this supercomputer. The brain is much more complex as each of our two billion neurons are connected to each other through infinite pathways. Nerve impulses traverse infinitely fast owing to the action of neurotransmitters. It doesn't take time for our brain to register touch, taste, sight, and smell. It is instant and automatic.

Now add the human body, soul and consciousness and we get something more powerful than the human brain—the human mind. Even in the 21st century, the human mind is as mysterious to scientists as it was during the middle ages. No scientific thinker can provide a rational explanation as to why certain people who are positive minded get cured of cancer, whereas others succumb to it. Other unsolvable mysteries of the human mind, include the power of prophetic dreams, ESP (extra sensory perception), instant and complete memorisation of medical encyclopaedias, super reading speeds and telekinesis.

It has been scientifically proved that the number of neuron interconnections in the brain may exceed the number of molecules in our universe. This proves that human beings are utilising only a fraction of the infinite power of the mind. Psychoanalysts have taken help of Indian medical texts like the *Charaka Samhita* to unravel the mysteries of the human mind. Western scientific thinking has come out of brain research and have moved to mind research. Their research findings indicate that the human mind can be sub-divided into three distinct areas. Seven per cent of the human mind is conscious. We use a fraction of our conscious mind for our day-to-day activities. Geniuses like Albert Einstein used more of their conscious mind as compared with the average man.

The layer just below the conscious mind is called the subconscious mind. Thirty-eight percent of the human mind is in the subconscious. All memories from birth are stored in the subconscious using an advanced filing system. It is possible to awaken the subconscious mind by putting the conscious mind to sleep. Hypnosis works at the subconscious level as the hypnotist puts the conscious mind to sleep either through progressive relaxation or by inducing a mild trance through a

pendulum or other hypnotic objects. Hypnotic sugges-
tions at subconscious levels are known to have worked
for people struggling to give up habits like smoking or
alcoholism.

The largest and least understood layer of the mind
lies below the subconscious and is termed as unconscious. Fifty-five per cent of the human mind lies in the
unconscious. This psycho-analytical theory of the mind
is also known as the iceberg theory, as the human mind
is compared to an iceberg, where only a small fraction
is visible but the larger fraction is submerged and hence
invisible. Now, as 55 per cent of the human mind is in
the unconscious, techniques to empower the mind
should focus on this area.

As explained, earlier, if the neurons are mini-silicon
chips of our brain, it is possible to get the desired output
by programming them. This is very true of the unconscious mind, however unlike a computer, the human
brain cannot be programmed by any computer pro-
grammer who works on the machine. It can only be
programmed by the owner and that is yourself.

Just as the computer works on electricity, the human
brain works on glucose. However, the brain has this
uncanny ability to recognise the glucose molecules that
give it energy. Glucose molecules that are metabolised
from natural sources like vegetables, grains and fruits are
the ideal source of power, while we programme our
unconscious mind. Thus, a healthy vegetarian diet is as
useful to the body as it is to the mind. Therefore, it is

advisable to begin programming only after you are confident of changing over to a simple, balanced vegetarian diet for six weeks before you start implementing these tips to improve your mind power.

As the unconscious is buried deep in the human psyche, any attempt to communicate with the unconscious has to begin by bypassing the conscious and subconscious levels. One of the simplest ways to do this is to use mind power music. This music is like software. They will work for you only if the same is compatible with your hardware. You may try different kinds of music, till you find the one which works best for you. The strains of soothing music calms the body and helps it relax. At the same time, it puts your conscious and unconscious minds to sleep till you reach the delta state. At delta state, you are ready to start programming your super computer. The *delta state* is reached when you close your eyes, roll your eyeballs upwards, take three deep breaths and touch the roof of your throat with the tongue. At this state, the unconscious mind becomes ready to accept programming commands. In other words, you are now ready to write your javascript!

There are certain techniques that you can use to programme your unconscious mind to get positive outcomes. These include creative visualisation, auto-suggestion and Zen meditation among several others. If you are going for a job interview, visualise a positive outcome before you go to the venue. Keep watching a movie of it in the theatre of your mind. Whatever the mind conceives and believes, it achieves. If you would like to overcome a health disability, keep talking to yourself by constantly repeating, 'I am getting healthier and healthier.' Meditation is a powerful way to reach delta level. Dynamic meditation and Zen meditation have proved to be especially useful for goal achievement among managers. One of the important benefits of the human mind is that it can be programmed with equal efficiency irrespective of age. A 60-year-old man or a teenager can get identical results if they use these techniques of empowerment with regularity. What are you waiting for? Discover the power of your unconscious mind today. The *answer* lies in your hands.

chapter 10

learning is fun in ZeNLP

A physics professor is struggling to explain the theory of relativity to his class. The blackboard is full of mathematical formulas and explanations. Innumerable chalkmarks dot the blackboard which looks more white than black. However, the students are as ignorant about Einstein's theory as they were at the start of the lecture, a couple of hours ago. This is how traditional teaching approaches the theory of relativity. A simple theory is made difficult until either students walk out in disgust or doze off in boredom.

Here is how we explain the theory of relativity in ZeNLP workshops:

Once upon a time on an island off the coast of Kerala, lived two monkeys—one white and the other black. Both monkeys had identical wristwatches. The watches were synchronised to show exactly the same time. At noon, the white monkey was made to sit on a rocket and hurtled into space at the speed of light, whereas the black monkey remained on the island. After one hour, the wristwatches of both monkeys were examined. It was found that the black monkey's watch showed a time of 1:00 p.m. as expected. However, the white monkey's watch showed a time of 12:30 p.m. This proved that time is not absolute but becomes relative when one travels at the speed of light. In other words, time slows down when one travels at the speed of light. This is the theory of relativity as propounded by Albert Einstein.

Now, which method of learning did you enjoy? The conventional learning through mathematical formulas and logical deductions or the story about the two monkeys? We are sure we know your answer. Hundreds of participants at our ZeNLP workshops have given us feedback that they prefer to learn through the language of stories. Stories teach adults that learning can be fun. They touch the emotions, are easy to recall and make learning a joyous experience. Thus, stories are powerful tools to create change and spread fast, as exemplified by the anecdote, which follows.

One day a young lad finds a lamp in his attic. This ancient lamp is covered with dust and soot. There is an inscription on the lamp which cannot be read due to the thick soot deposited on it. The lad rubs the lamp gently expecting the proverbial genie to emerge, but his efforts are to no avail. Remembering the Chinese adage which says, 'Don't curse darkness but light a lamp to dispel it', the lad lights the lamp and begins to make shadows of animals with his hands, playing on the reflections of his fingers. Soon, he masters the art of shadow play and invites the children of his village and entertains them with his skilful fingers. children are enthralled and request him to teach them this art. The lad teaches these children the fine art of making shadows of birds, dogs, cats and squirrels. A few weeks later this young lad leaves his village and travels far and wide with his magic lamp.

A few months later, he arrives at a village hundreds of miles away from his native village and sees a huge crowd around a candle-lit tent. He gently asks one of the villagers about the event. He comes to know that the crowd had gathered to witness a first-hand display of shadow play. Merging into the crowd, the young lad finds himself seeing the same shadow tricks he had taught the children at his native village.

The next morning, he takes his lamp to the river and scrubs it clean with coconut husks. Finally, all the soot and dust disappears and he is able to read the tiny inscription on the lamp. It reads, 'What is invisible, spreads fast and spreads warmth and joy? Can you think of the answer to this question? Think for a minute. The answer is knowledge!

Knowledge is invisible, knowledge spreads fast and knowledge spreads warmth and joy.

Learning is fun when teachers use the language of stories, anecdotes, proverbs, folk tales, parables and mythological tales. Learning becomes fun when students continue to pay attention long after the session ends. Learning is fun when students learn while playing games. The most important equipment at ZeNLP workshops are whistles, balloons and toys. Use of notepads, pens and pencils are prohibited. Participants are encouraged to leave the classroom if they find the sessions boring. Instructors seldom use chalk or blackboards. Rapport is created between the tutor and pupils through regular sessions of brief but energetic physical exercise. Every session ends with a brief relaxation routine to recharge energies through Nidra meditation.

The morning sessions begin with prayers and evening sessions end with chanting of hymns from the Geeta, psalms from the Bible and *kalmas* from the Koran. Participants are motivated to gently close their eyelids and absorb the lessons unconsciously. Experience teaches us that over the last five years, more than 3000 participants have attended ZeNLP workshops and most of them are able to remember and recall the stories we narrate during our workshops. Most participants remember the Desert Survival Game, Cave Rescue Game, Communication Game, Numbers Game and Housies we played as it was a new and unique experience for them.

Our experience proves that learning can be permanent without the use of pens, chalk, blackboards and notepads if one uses the language of stories and games. ZeNLP (Neurolinguistic Programming with a touch of Zen) shows you the way to learn creatively and teaches managers that management development programmes can be made fun through innovative learning techniques.

chapter 11

improving memory using ZeNLP

An old Zen master always told this fable to his students: Late one night a blind man was about to go home after visiting a friend. 'Please,' he said to his friend, 'may I take your lantern with me?' 'Why carry a lantern?' asked his friend. 'You won't see any better with it.' 'No,' said the blind one, 'perhaps not. But others will see me better, and not bump into me.' So his friend gave the blind man the lantern, which was made of paper on bamboo strips, with a candle inside. Off went the blind man with the lantern, and before he had gone more than a few yards, 'Crack!'—a traveller walked right into him. The blind man was very angry. 'Why don't you look out?' he stormed. 'Don't you see this lantern?' 'Why don't you light the candle?' asked the traveller.

There is a great truth hidden behind this simple Zen story. Only a minute fraction of humanity understands the incredible power of the human mind. These enlightened souls are the blind men who have lit their candles. In India, we know them as *hatha-yogis*, who can sleep on beds of nails, walk through fire and even stop their heartbeat. The vast majority of human beings are like the blind man in the Zen story. You have not yet discovered the hidden power of your unconscious mind. ZeNLP is a tool to discover your hidden powers.

ZeNLP is the new technology of achievement to improve memory and concentration, create rapport, reduce stress, build confidence and develop a positive mental attitude. ZeNLP uses simple visualisation techniques, auto-suggestions and metaphors in the way our brain codes information. To give you an idea of the simplicity and effectiveness of ZeNLP techniques, a few simple techniques to remember names is elucidated. You can practise these techniques and the results will convince you that you can programme your brain using creative visualisation, auto-suggestion and dynamic meditation.

When was the last time you saw someone whose name you should have remembered? They knew you and called you by name. But you had no idea what their name was. Imagine how wonderful it would be if you could always remember a person's name after you met them. It would certainly save you future embarrassment.

Here is an easy and practical way of remembering names. Using this ZeNLP name strategy, you can learn and remember the names of 30 or more people in less than 30 minutes. We demonstrate this in our ZeNLP workshops. At the beginning of each workshop, all students introduce themselves and afterwards they can recall everyone's name. Not only are the students' names installed into each other's short-term memories, but in their long-term memories as well. If you meet a person just once, you can usually remember their name for a long time by using this strategy.

We developed this name strategy by studying the thinking processes of people who remembered names well. Franklin D. Roosevelt, one of the people we studied, was a master at recalling names. He continually amazed his staff by remembering someone's name that he had only met once, months before. Asked how he did it, he said he saw the person's name written out on their forehead.

We expanded the version of Roosevelt's name strategy in ZeNLP workshops. This name strategy is based on the way people learn and recall information, which is through the three primary senses of sight, sound and touch. These are the ZeNLP classification of individuals into visuals, auditories and kinesthetics based on their preferred mental maps. One of the things that brain researchers have discovered in the last few years is that your internal dialogue occupies the same auditory nerve in your ear as external sound.

The reason why people forget names is because they're usually involved in some other auditory, internal conversation. So, it is really hard to hear the other person saying their name when you're having an internal conversation with yourself about how you're coming across or what you're going to say next.

In remembering names, the first thing that we recommend is to concentrate on staying external with the person by listening to them. Then repeat their name to yourself three times while you're looking at them.

To get the visual part in, imagine that you can see their name written on their forehead. To make it more permanent, see their name in your favourite colour. This will make it stick out all the better. Do this while you're saying their names to yourself.

The third way to remember a person's name is through the kinesthetic sense of 'touch'. You can code this in by letting your finger imagine what it would be like to write the person's name as you're seeing it and saying it to yourself. You can also move your finger in little micro-muscle movements as if you were actually writing their name. This will code their name into your neurology at a more deeper level.

You can try these three techniques and find out which one works for you. Or, you could get an analysis of your ZeNLP preferred mental map done and we can tell you which technique will work best for you.

If you use this process with everyone you meet, pretty soon it will become an automatic part of who you are and you'll just do it unconsciously whenever you meet someone new. This is a simple ZeNLP technique which works like magic. You can practise this technique and email your feedback to us at zenlp@rediffmail.com.

This will convince you that ZeNLP works. This name strategy also comes in handy when you meet a large group of people for the first time. The process that I use to remember large groups of names is called 'chunking', which is the art of breaking down information into smaller pieces.

Most people learn information by chunking it down. Think about your credit card number. That's one big number. Now break it down into three small chunks. You will remember the chunks faster than the big number. Telephone numbers are the same way, you remember them by breaking them down into two chunks of numbers.

When it comes to remembering large groups of people, we chunk everyone's name into groups of five. You can do this by having the five people say their names to you and then repeat their names back as you code each one of them into your memory through your preferred mental map.

People are always asking me how come I can remember so many names. The reason is rather simple; I've had lots of practice. I encourage my students to practise this memory technique as often as possible. In reality, anyone can do this process. If it's done the way we teach it, you'll find that you can remember a large group of people's names with ease, and you'll be able to remember people's names forever.

chapter 12

creativity in ZeNLP

What is creativity?

Creativity is unconscious competence in action. Unconscious competence is the fine art of achieving excellence in any field with minimum effort. Creativity is taking the path of least resistance and working with, rather than against, the universal laws of nature. Creative managers have the ability to tap into the cosmic consciousness or universal consciousness and align themselves to be in tune with this universal force.

A student physicist Heinz Maier Leibnitz suggested a new way to represent on the blackboard, the behaviour of a subatomic particle. Maier agreed as the new formulation was an improvement of the earlier one. Years later, this student went on to win the Nobel Prize in Physics.

Just as the sound of a tree crashing in the forest is unheard if nobody is there to hear it, so creative ideas vanish unless there is a receptive audience to record and implement them. Creativity is not a spark. Rather creativity is a flow. It is more like a flowing river and less like the flash of lightning. But how do we ensure that creativity flows in our actions?

Any activity becomes a flow of creativity, if it meets the following criterion:

There are clear goals every step of the way

Creativity should flow and, in the flow, we always know what needs to be done next. The musician knows what notes to play next, the rock climber knows the next moves to make. Creative people have clear goals.

There is an immediate feedback to one's actions

In a flow of experience, we know how well we are doing. The musician hears right away whether the note played is the right one. The rock climber knows immediately whether his move was correct because he is still hanging out there.

There is a balance between challenges and skills

In flow, we feel that our abilities are matched to the opportunities for action. Playing chess with a stronger opponent leads to frustration, while playing chess with a much weaker opponent leads to boredom. In a really enjoyable game, the players are balanced on a fine line between boredom and anxiety. The same is true for creativity. There has to be a balance. The task must not be too difficult or too easy.

Action and awareness are merged

Sitting in a class, students may appear to be paying attention to the teacher, but they may actually be thinking about lunch. But in flow, our concentration is focused on what we do.

Distractions are excluded

In flow, you are aware of only what is relevant. Like Arjuna could see only the eye of the bird he was shooting; nothing else. If the musician thinks of his tax problems while playing, he is more likely to hit a wrong note. Avoid distractions.

There is no fear of failure

While in flow, we are too involved to be concerned with failure. The issue of failure doesn't crop up when you are in full flow.

Self-consciousness disappears

The musician feels in harmony with the cosmos. The athlete moves one with the team. The reader transports himself to virtual reality. There is self-forgetfulness when you are in creative flow.

Time sense becomes distorted

Generally in flow, we forget time and hours may flow in what seems like a few minutes. Our sense of how time passes is dictated by what we are doing.

Thus, we can bring a creative flow into our activities through one-pointedness of the mind, close match between challenges and skills. All this is made possible by clarity of goals and the constant availability of feedback. One should be able to accomplish the task effortlessly, and failure doesn't exist. Time is non-existent and the act, stage and actor become one. You can experience creativity by listening to Beethoven's best symphonies which were composed when he was deaf. Or, you could see floral paintings made by Mouth and Foot painting artists, all of whom are quadriplegics.

chapter 13

the power of dreams in ZeNLP

One day a Zen master entered his favourite teahouse and said: 'The moon is more useful than the sun'. An old man asked, 'Why?' The master replied, 'We need the light more during the night than during the day.'

There is a great truth hidden behind this simple Zen story. ZeNLP research has shown that what we dream is often more useful than what we do during our waking hours. An average man sleeps for seven to eight hours every day. This means we spend one-third of our lives sleeping! And almost every night, we see dreams. We do not remember all our dreams, but Rapid Eye Movement (REM) analysis has proved that we see several dreams each night. REM sleep is a phase of shallow sleep that occurs several times during a night. It is so called because our eyes flicker rapidly during this time. During our four or five cycles of REM or dreaming sleep each night, we experience between 60 to 90 minutes of dreamtime. Some dreams also occur outside of REM phases of sleep.

Ancient Egyptian, Mayan, Incan, Tibetan and Vedic scriptures have emphasised the hidden power of our dreams. The Upanishads say that the waking state represents the conscious mind, the sleeping state represents the subconscious mind while the dream state represents the unconscious mind. As 7 per cent of mind is conscious, 38 per cent is subconscious and 55 per cent is in the unconscious, techniques to empower the mind should focus on the unconscious! This evidently means that dreams are much more powerful than previously imagined to be. As the focus of ZeNLP is to empower the unconscious mind through creative visualisation, auto-suggestion and dynamic meditation, recording and analysis of dreams becomes a critical area.

ZeNLP research, based on analysis of dream diaries of participants who attended our workshops, tell us that dreams have been given to us for our benefit. We are spiritual beings and we have the potential to experience many different levels of awareness while in the dream state from which we may gain insights into all aspects of our life: physical, mental, and spiritual. Dreams can help us diagnose health problems, encourage us in the decisions we make, or reprimand us for negative behaviour in our relationships. They can be instructive and practical, light-hearted fun or spiritually uplifting, depending on what we need most at a given time. Even major life issues are addressed in dreams; in fact, nothing of importance happens to us without it first having been foreshadowed in our dreams.

Although dreams often contain symbols of a universal or archetypal nature with similar meanings in diverse cultures, ZeNLP stresses the highly individual nature of dreams. In order to begin utilising our dream insights fully, the dreamer may decide on a course of action in order to make use of the dream insight. Perhaps a change in attitude is required, or maybe circumstances can be seen from a new perspective and the individual decides to adopt a different approach to the issue. Once the dreamer arrives at a basic understanding of the dream and takes some action based on that information, then a growth process begins which allows the dreamer to reach a deeper and clearer level of insight from which to proceed.

Since 1995, when we started conducting ZeNLP workshops to increase the effectiveness and efficiency of managers, thousands of managers who have attended our workshops have been recording and emailing their dream diaries to us. These managers also set their personal and organisational goals at these workshops. We regularly monitor their progress towards the goals set by them and compare it with their dream diaries to establish a co-relation. An in-depth analysis of this vast resource of information reveals interesting results. Managers who have maintained their dream diaries found that their major achievements including promotions, transfers and achievements were pre-shadowed in their dream diaries.

Thus, study of dreams can help us develop to our highest potential. The rewards of that endeavour is well worth our time and effort. ZeNLP workshops help participants discover the hidden power in their dreams and to employ them effectively to multiply their mind power manifold.

Sigmund Freud (1865–1939) began the work of understanding dreams in the modern era. He rejected the idea that dreams were a response to events outside ourselves. Freud believed that at the heart of our dreams lies our deepest desires which our dreams keep hidden from our waking minds. Carl Gustav Jung (1875–1961) disagreed with Freud by arguing that dreams were vital messages designed to be listened to, not hidden away. Jung was convinced that dreams help to reveal to our waking minds many of our deepest wishes and, by doing so, help us fulfil our ambitions.

Remember: Everything and everyone in your dream is a part of you, from the shadow in the corner to the flowers in the background to the paper on which a letter was written. Take time out to discover what each symbol means and you will discover a lot about yourself. Dreams help us resolve problems, face fears and indulge in passions. Therefore, it is no coincidence that your dreams almost always feature people, places and situations about which you have strong feelings. The right side of the brain is responsible for creativity and imagery, while the left side is concerned with rational and analytical thinking. You may expect, therefore, that dreaming takes place in the right side, but this is not true. The left side can also dream, although these dreams are less symbolic and less imaginative.

A Zen teaching story tells of a man who prayed continually for the awareness to succeed in life. Then one night he dreamed of going into the forest to attain understanding. The next morning he went into the woods and wandered for several hours looking for some sign that would provide answers. When he finally stopped to rest, he saw a fox with no legs lying between two rocks in a cool place. Curious as to how a legless fox could survive, he waited until sunset when he observed a lion come and lay meat before the fox. 'Ah, I understand,' the man thought. 'The secret to success in life is to trust that God will take care of all my needs. I don't need to provide for myself. All I have to do is totally surrender to my all-sustaining God.' Two weeks later, weakened and starving, the man had another dream. In it he heard a voice say, 'Fool. Be like the lion, not like the fox.'

chapter 14

evolution of communication

It was over 35,000 years ago that man first displayed his talent for communication. Our ancestors began by painting or etching figures on the cave wall with the help of ivory and bone. Even today, archaeologists have discovered cave-man paintings in Europe and Africa. Some of these paintings were carbon-dated to have been etched during the pre-historic age. From these primitive paintings, man evolved to formulate a language of pictures as exemplified by Egyptian hieroglyphics. Ancient Chinese and even the Harrapans used pictography to communicate.

Six thousand years ago, man discovered the use of clay tablets for writing. This was probably the earliest known system of written communication. It was widely used by the Sumericans, Babylonians and Assyrians. From clay tablets, man began to use animal hide to record written communication. Some of the world's most ancient writings are preserved in tender lamb or calf skin, even today. The Bible, Greek classics and Roman Law were written on tender lamb or calf skin (Vellum). The next evolution in written communication came from India. Handed over from generation to generation, the Vedas, Upanishads, Ramayana and Mahabharata are some of the outstanding examples of teaching and epics. These epics were transcribed on lotus leaves, *bhoj patras* or on dried palm tree leaves. Even today, horoscopes in Kerala continue to be etched on dried leaves with a sharp point.

The next step in the evolution of communication came with the discovery of paper. Egyptians perfected the art of writing on papyrus—the reedy water plant. Events like religious festivals, wars and natural calamities were recorded on papyrus. Then, in the year BC 100, the Chinese invented paper. Man has tried over 400 different materials to perfect the art of making paper. Jute, rags, bamboo, wood and numerous other materials have been tried and tested to make the perfect paper. By the 15th century AD, paper emerged as the single most important medium of man's written communication. The invention of mechanical printing by Guttenberg in 1455 AD heralded the modern age of paper and printing.

But even in this modern age, some tribes continue to use indigenous modes of communication, which have survived till date and continue to be reliable. Long before Christopher Columbus or Amerigo Vespucci discovered America, native Red Indian tribes had mastered the art of communication through smoke signals. They used it extensively in war and peace. Even today, the Hopi Indians of North America use smoke signals as a means of warning against impending natural calamities like floods. Mass evacuations are possible at split second speeds owing to the efficacy of this unique means of communication. The notation system in music owes its origins to the Incas of Peru. The ancient Incans made musical notations in a form of knots on a string called 'Quipu'. Coloured knots were used to add different meanings. Even today the Peruvian Indians continue to use this traditional mode of communication. Closer home, tribals in the Simlipal forests in Orissa use drumbeats to communicate. Subtle differences in the tone, volume, pitch, bass and timbre of the drumbeat are effectively used to communicate birth, death, festivity, community gatherings, danger, harvest, weather forecasts and other important events of importance to their society. During the Mughal period, pigeons were used to deliver written communication to recipients. Arabs used falcons for the same purpose. Greeks used athletes to deliver written communication.

The invention of the typewriter, telephone, television, telegraph, video cassette players, cameras, motion pictures, audio-players and other gadgets gave a boost to spoken, written and visual communication and the 1900s became the age of communication. Soon, spool tapes gave way to compact audio tapes. Audio tapes made way to compact discs and compact discs to digital voice devices. The typewriter was replaced by the computer, telephones gave way to cellphones and paper is being replaced by cyberspace. With computers connected through telephone cables, a network of computers was created, aptly named the Internet. The Internet spread its tentacles a hundred times faster than telephone and five times faster than television to reach a billion earthlings. By 2020, every third earthling will have access to Internet. This is the forecast of tips4ceos.com, an Internet advisory dotcom for Pharmaceutical CEOs. Email has replaced telephones and telegrams. The speed of this cyber-revolution is so fast that a year is measured by Internet companies in days. In the near future, a minute on the Internet would become equivalent to a normal year, if cyber-pandits spell out their vision of the future. Millions of software engineers spend endless hours writing billions of lines of code in an effort to keep ahead in the race to dominate the Net.

Man had started living in the communication millennium. It was Henry Miller who said, 'In expanding the field of knowledge we but increase the horizon of ignorance' This quote assumes a great significance when taken in context of the so-called communication revolution of today. The basic fact that the Internet enables human beings to communicate, has been forgotten. The Net is nothing more than a convenient means of communication and serves us no better than the smoke signals serve Red Indians. In a bid to get ahead in the technological race, humanity has ignored the greatest communication tool in this universe and that is the human mind. After all, it was the human mind that invented the Net and all these modern-day gadgets of communication. Mankind has forgotten to explore pathways of expanding the infinite potential of the human mind. Henry Miller's saying is exemplified by my true life experience.

A few years ago, I happened to be sitting next to a group of German agricultural scientists who were flying to Bhubaneshwar for a research project. One of the scientists informed me that they were trying to find a solution to reduce wastage of foodgrain in their fields in Germany from birds. They had tried all modern techniques including round-the-clock security guards shooting rubber bullets, ultrasonic vibrations, frequency jammers and radars in an effort to repulse the birds but had failed and they ended up with weary-eyed security guards in addition to reduced harvests. They had even visited Australia and trained their guards on the use of boomerangs, but to no avail. Finally, a non-resident Indian had suggested him to try Orissa.

I accompanied these scientists to the interior tribal villages in Orissa and learnt a lot about their methods of agriculture and medicine. Once, while spending the night on a machan (tree-house), we could hear the continuous clanging of a bell throughout the night. Spending a sleepless night we decided to pay a visit to the tribals who were the source of our disturbance. As we neared the source of the sound, we found no tribals around. Instead of finding a tribal ringing the bell, we found ourselves at the edge of a perennial mountain stream. The tribals had built a contraption out of bamboo, which was placed in the path of the waterfall. As the water hit this contraption, a see-saw mechanism saw the free end of the bamboo swinging wildly. Attached to it was a large metal bell. As long as the water kept falling on the bamboo contraption, the bell continued to clang. As this was a perennial waterfall, the bell clanged throughout the day and night, thus scaring away the birds, which preyed on their crops. And soon, the Germans had their solution to their own crisis. They employed a windmill to create an artificial perennial stream near their fields and used the tribal bamboo contraption and bell to scare away the winged predators throughout the harvest season, thus saving them millions of tons of grain. The admirable quality among the Germans was their ability and willingness to learn. Here I would like to quote Eric Hoffer, who said, 'It is the malady of our information technology age that the young are so busy teaching us that they have no time left to learn.'

The Divine Pymander says, 'The union of the word and the mind produces that mystery which is called life...Learn deeply of the mind and its mystery, for therein lies the secret of immortality.' Unfortunately, most modern-day research is focussed on the brain, not on the mind. Scientists are more interested in the neuro-chemistry of the brain rather than in the telepathic capabilities of mind. Scientific thinking has become imprisoned by the speed of light. Communication can evolve further only after man acknowledges his spiritual origins and explores the possibility of time travel by expansion of consciousness through regular meditation.

Can mind communicate to mind? Isn't their scientific proof of extra sensory perception? Can man communicate through thoughts alone? Is astral travel a reality? The next revolution in the field of wireless communication can only happen after the world starts a scientific journey to unravel the unexplored potential of the human mind. Otherwise, one will be deserted in the middle of the debates on the demands for greater bandwidth, higher gigabytes of hard disk capacity and more random access memory (RAM).

chapter 15

tree plantation meditation in ZeNLP

A crow was sitting on a tree, doing nothing all day. A small rabbit saw the crow and asked him: 'Can I also sit like you and do nothing all day long?' The crow answered: 'Sure, why not?' So, the rabbit sat on the ground below the crow, and rested. All of a sudden, a fox appeared, jumped on the rabbit and ate him up. Then the crow thought: 'Poor rabbit, I forgot to tell him that if you want to do nothing, you must sit very high....'

Since ancient days, Vedic Aryans have been worshipping trees. Be it the humble *tulsi* plant or the mighty banyan tree. Worshipping of trees continues to this day in several villages in India. There is a scientific reason behind tree worship. The increased oxygen content in air results in health benefits for the villagers participating in these day-long ceremonies. Trees absorb carbon dioxide during the day and release oxygen. As the entire village collects under trees, it generates a sense of community feeling. Environment consciousness is created among villagers as the tree is worshipped as a goddess. Tree worship is ZeNLP Meditation in the truest sense.

ZeNLP exercises teach us the subtle art of maintaining harmony with nature and to vibrate with the cosmic energy of this universe. The word universe is a combination of uni + verse. Uni means one and verse means song. Thus, the word universe means 'One Song' and ZeNLP meditation teaches us the subtle art of singing this song by vibrating with the energies of this universe.

Every tree is a symbol of the oneness of the cosmic world. Trees are the embodiment of the elements of ZeNLP—Fire, Water and Earth. Trees are rooted in the earth element, need sunlight (Fire element) for photosynthesis and need the Water element for their healthy growth. All trees need these elements and, hence, tree plantation meditation becomes a powerful technique to align our energy in tune with the cosmic energy and to help us overcome disease which is a manifestation of the imbalance in cosmic energy.

In the ancient days, tree plantation meditation was the only source of healing and ancient texts like Rig Veda and Upanishads talk about the curative properties of trees, leaves, roots, herbs and flowers. Even to this day, most medicines are directly or indirectly sourced from plants.

Each person has an energy affinity to a particular tree and this is based on the time of his birth. The exact tree that needs to be planted depends on the diseased person's birth date, energy patterns and disease. However, healthy individuals can also benefit by planting trees. Managers can plant trees (according to the chart mentioned below) to maintain a positive mental attitude, retain positive ethereal energy and to be successful at the workplace. In ZeNLP workshops the exact location of planting the tree and the ceremonies that needed to be carried out are elucidated in minute detail so that all participants can energise their personal, family and business life by tree plantation meditation.

Based on the preferred mental maps of the managers, saplings are selected for plantation. These include Gulmohar saplings for visuals, Ashoka saplings for auditories and Neem saplings for kinesthetics. Managers are encouraged to work as a team and prepare the soil for plantations. The soil is dug-out with spades and pick-axes. A sufficient gap is maintained between each tree and this meditation is conducted in the early hours of the morning.

Managers gently place the sapling in its designated place and cover it with clods of earth picked by their own hand. They collect water by cupping their hands and pour it over the sapling three times. Later, they face the morning sun, close their eyelids and complete their

ZeNLP visualisation exercises. All managers solemnly affirm they will visit the sapling daily and give it water ensuring its growth. They also pledge to practise their ZeNLP visualisation exercises whenever they visit the tree and maintain their dream diary. They also pray to the cosmic energy to propel them towards their individual, family and career goals set at the workshop.

Which tree are you? Which tree does your birthday fall under?

Dates	Tree (*Indian Equivalent*)
December 23 to January 1	Apple tree (*Seb*)
January 2 to January 11	Fir tree (*Chickoo*)
January 12 to January 24	Elm tree (*Neem*)
January 25 to February 3	Cypress tree (*Peepal*)
February 4 to February 8	Poplar tree (*Coconut*)
February 9 to February 18	Cedar tree (*Mango*)
February 19 to February 28	Pine tree (*Peru*)
March 1 to March 10	Weeping willow tree (*Ashoka*)
March 11 to March 20	Lime tree (*Nimbu*)
March 21	Oak tree (*Silver oak*)
March 22 to March 31	Hazelnut tree (*Bilva*)
April 1 to April 10	Rowan tree (*Jack fruit*)
April 11 to April 20	Maple tree (*Sitaphal*)
April 21 to April 30	Walnut tree (*Akrot*)
May 1 to May 14	Poplar tree (*Coconut*)
May 15 to May 24	Chestnut tree (*Guava*)
May 25 to June 3	Ash tree (*Tamarind*)

June 4 to June 13	Hornbeam tree (*Rain tree*)
June 14 to June 23	Fig tree (*Papaya*)
June 24	Birch tree (*Gulmohar*)
June 25 to July 4	Apple tree (*Seb*)
July 5 to July 14	Fir tree (*Chickoo*)
July 15 to July 25	Elm tree (*Neem*)
July 26 to August 4	Cypress tree (*Peepal*)
August 5 to August 14	Poplar tree (*Coconut*)
August 15 to August 23	Cedar tree (*Mango*)
August 24 to September 2	Pine tree (*Peru*)
September 3 to September 12	Weeping willow tree (*Ashoka*)
September 13 to September 22	Lime tree (*Nimbu*)
September 23	Olive tree (*Amla*)
September 24 to October 3	Hazelnut tree (*Bilva*)
October 4 to October 13	Rowan tree (*Jack fruit*)
October 14 to October 23	Maple tree (*Sitaphal*)
October 24 to November 11	Walnut tree (*Akrot*)
November 12 to November 21	Chestnut tree (*Guava*)
November 22 to December 1	Ash tree (*Tamarind*)
December 2 to December 11	Hornbeam tree (*Rain tree*)
December 12 to December 21	Fig tree (*Papaya*)
December 22	Birch tree (*Gulmohar*)

Tree plantation meditation is a powerful ZeNLP technique which has the power to cure diseases and to forge a stronger bond with the elements. It all depends on the way you look at things.

One day a father and his rich family took his son to a trip to the country with the firm purpose to show him how poor people can be. They spent a day and a night in the farm of a very poor family. When they returned from their trip, the father asked his son, 'How was the trip?' 'Very good, Dad!' 'Did you see how poor people can be?' the father asked. 'Yeah!' 'And what did you learn?' The son answered, 'I saw that we have a dog at home, and they have four. We have a pool that reaches to the middle of the garden, they have creek that has no end. We have imported lamps in the garden, they have the stars. Our patio reaches to the front yard, they have a whole horizon.' When the little boy was finishing, his father was speechless. His son added, 'Thanks Dad for showing me how poor we are!'

chapter 16

which is your healing tree?

Four monks decided to meditate silently without speaking for two weeks. By nightfall on the first day, the candle began to flicker and then went out. The first monk said, 'Oh, no! The candle is out.' The second monk said, 'Aren't we not supposed to talk?' The third monk said, 'Why must you two break the silence?' The fourth monk laughed and said, 'Ha! I'm the only one who didn't speak.

There is a deep meaning behind this simple Zen story. According to Zen, each tree represents a human being and has specific physical, mental and spiritual characteristics. Every human being can strengthen these characteristics through ZeNLP meditation and tree-plantation ceremonies.

The tree is a metaphor which represents certain fundamental truths and these metaphors are more by design than by accident. Consider the following trees and the type of person the tree represents. By reading this exhaustive list, you can analyse the tree that represents you.

Apple tree represents love

Of slight build, lots of charm, appeal and attraction, pleasant aura, flirtatious, adventurous, sensitive, always in love, wants to live and be loved, faithful and tender partner, very generous, scientific talents, lives for today, a carefree philosopher with imagination.

Fir tree represents the mysterious

Extraordinary taste, dignity, cultivated airs, loves anything beautiful, moody, stubborn, tends towards egoism but cares for those close to it, rather modest, very ambitious, talented, industrious, many friends, many foes, very reliable.

Elm tree represents noble-mindedness

Pleasant shape, tasteful clothes, modest demands, tends to not forgive mistakes, cheerful, likes to lead but not to obey, honest and faithful partner, tends to a know-all-attitude and making decisions for others, noble-minded, generous, good sense of humour, practical.

Conifers represent faithfulness

Strong, muscular, adaptable, takes what life has to give, happy, content, optimistic, needs enough money and acknowledgement, hates loneliness, passionate lover who cannot be satisfied, faithful, quick-tempered, unruly, pedantic and careless.

Mango tree represents uncertainty

Looks very decorative, self-confident, only courageous if necessary, needs goodwill and pleasant surroundings, very choosy, often lonely, great animosity, artistic nature, good organiser, tends to be philosophical, reliable in any situation, takes partnership seriously.

Asopalav (Ashoka) represents confidence

Of rare beauty, knows how to adapt, likes luxury, of good health, not in the least shy, tends to look down on others, self-confident, determined, impatient, wants to impress others, many talents, industrious, healthy optimism, waiting for the one true love, able to make quick decisions.

Pine tree represents particularity

Loves agreeable company, very robust, knows how to make life comfortable, very active, natural, good companion, but seldom friendly, falls easily in love but its passion burns out quickly, gives up easily, many disappointments till it finds its ideal, trustworthy, practical.

Rubber tree represents melancholy

Beautiful but full of melancholy, attractive, very empathic, loves anything beautiful and tasteful, loves to travel, dreamer, restless, capricious, honest, can be influenced but is not easy to live with, demanding, good intuition, suffers in love but an anchoring partner.

Lime tree represents doubt

Accepts what life dishes out in a composed way, hates fighting, stress and labour, likes laziness and idleness, soft and relenting, makes sacrifices for friends, many talents but not tenacious enough to make them blossom, often wailing and complaining, very jealous, loyal.

Coconut tree represents the extraordinary

Charming, undemanding, very understanding, knows how to make an impression, active fighter for social causes, popular, moody and capricious lover, honest and tolerant partner, precise sense of judgement.

Tamarind tree represents sensitivity

Full of charm, cheerful, gifted, without egoism, likes to draw attention, loves life, motion, unrest and even complications, is both dependent and independent, good taste, artistic, passionate, emotional, good company, does not forgive.

Neem tree represents independence of mind

No ordinary person, full imagination and originality, shy and reserved, ambitious, proud, lots of self-respect, hungers for new experiences, sometimes nervous, many complexes, good memory, learns easily, complicated love life, wants to impress.

Gulmohar tree represents passion

Unrelenting, strange and full of contrasts, often egoistic, aggressive, noble, broad horizon, unexpected reactions, spontaneous, unlimited ambition, no flexibility, difficult and uncommon partner, not always liked but often admired, ingenious strategist, very jealous and passionate, no compromises.

Banyan tree represents honesty

Of unusual beauty, does not want to impress, well-developed sense of justice, vivacious, interested, a born diplomat, but irritated and sensitive in company, lacks self-confidence, acts superior, feels not understood, loves only once, has difficulties in finding a partner.

Peepal tree represents ambition

Uncommonly attractive, vivacious, impulsive, demanding, does not care for criticism, ambitious, intelligent, talented, likes to play with fate, can be egoistic, very reliable and trustworthy, faithful and prudent lover, sometimes brain rules over heart, but takes partnership very seriously, cares for its looks and condition, good taste, makes life as comfortable as possible, leads reasonable, disciplined life, looks for kindness, an emotional partner and acknowledgement, dreams of unusual lovers, is seldom happy with its feelings, mistrusts most people, is never sure of its decisions, very conscientious.

Khajoor tree represents sensibility

Very strong, a bit self-willed, independent, does not allow contradiction or arguments, loves life, its family, children and animals, a bit of a butterfly, good sense of humour, likes idleness and laziness, of practical talent and intelligence.

Oak tree represents robust nature

Courageous, strong, unrelenting, independent, sensible, does not love changes, keeps its feet on the ground, person of action.

Teak tree represents inspiration

Vivacious, attractive, elegant, friendly, unpretentious, modest, does not like anything in excess, abhors the vulgar, loves life in nature, calm, not very passionate, full of imagination, little ambition, creates a calm and content atmosphere.

Amla tree represents wisdom

Loves sun, warmth and kind feelings, reasonable, balanced, avoids aggression and violence, tolerant, cheerful, calm, well-developed sense of justice, sensitive, empathic, free of jealousy, loves to read and likes the company of sophisticated people.

Chickoo tree represents the creative

Has good taste, concerned about its looks, materialist, good organisation of life and career, economical, good leader, takes no unnecessary risks, reasonable, splendid lifetime companion, keen on keeping fit.

Since 1995, when we started conducting ZeNLP workshops, several hundred managers have discovered the benefits of planting trees and forging a stronger bond with the elements. The cosmic consciousness, which lies dormant in the tail bone, can be activated through tree plantation ceremonies. Tree plantations are a part of holistic remedies and Canada's leading holistic remedy journal *Holier* includes tree plantations as a part of holistic therapy for terminally-ill cancer patients given up by medicine. *Holier* terms this therapy as 'horticulture therapy' and millions of Americans have discovered its benefits.

Patients have to plant a sapling, water it daily and treat it like a son or daughter. Here is a folk tale, recounted by the tribals of Baripada, on how the sal tree came to Orissa.

Long, long ago, the king of Mayurbhanj prayed for an offspring. Despite his prayers, he could not beget a son. He went to sages, medicants and fakirs but to no avail. Then one wise minister asked him to visit Sukra Dehuri, a tribal witch doctor inside the Simlipal forest. The king and his queen arrived at the tribal settlement and told Sukra about their predicament. Sukra conducted a tribal ritual, which blessed couples with fertility. Soon, Banga (the tribal deity) appeared before them, holding a sal sapling in his hands. He handed the sapling to Sukra Dehuri and disappeared.

*Sukra gave the sal sapling to the queen and asked her to
perform the following ceremony. The queen had to wake
up before sunrise, go to her garden and dig the earth with
her own hands and plant the sapling as the first rays of
sunlight were seen. She had to water the sapling, close her
eyes and visualise a newly born cherub. She had to repeat
this exercise every day at dawn and she would be blessed
by the birth of an offspring. The queen took the sapling in
her hand and promised to plant it in her garden and look
after it. The queen kept her promise and eventually gave
birth to a lovely daughter whom she named Shalu. Many
years later Shalu would play under the shadow of the sal
tree, which was planted by her mother before her birth.
Soon, the king ordered every married couple inside the forest
to plant a sal tree after their marriage. Soon, the hills were
covered with numerous sal trees and the sal forests that exist
around Baripada today are a result of the blessings of
Banga.*

Ashok Tandon, company secretary at Hindustan Aero-
nautics Ltd., planted an Ashoka tree in his garden in
Bangalore four years ago. Every morning, Tandon watered
and nurtured his tree. He was attracted to the Ashoka tree
from the day he planted it and the tree has grown faster
than the Ashoka trees planted by other participants in
their gardens on the same day.

Dr. B.N. Jayaprakash, medical officer at ITI hospital,
planted a rain-tree at ITI's factory in Bangalore four
years ago. He was attracted to the rain-tree from the day

he planted it and his tree has been growing rapidly. There are countless other examples from our workshops where participants were attracted to the tree they planted at our workshop and went on to plant several similar saplings at their homes and community gardens. One of our participants, Tarun Joshi, regularly conducts tree plantation camps at Rajashree Polyfils, after attending our workshop at Bharuch District Management Association.

ZeNLP meditation needs constant practice. Unless one waters and nurtures a sapling regularly, it will not grow. Similarly, a routine of constant practice helps one master ZeNLP, just as a routine of constant exercise builds strong bodies. The best aspect of ZeNLP is that the creative visualisation exercises and auto-suggestions can be practised while travelling, swimming, exercising or while you take your morning walk. One can listen to ZeNLP music for meditation at all times. The best time to practise ZeNLP meditation is just before drifting off to sleep at night. Late risers can laze around and complete the exercises in the morning while lying in bed.

ZeNLP is like a man hanging from a tree by his teeth over a precipice. His hands grasp no branch, his feet rest on no limb, and under the tree the Zen master asks him: 'Why did Buddha come to China from India?' if he does not answer, he fails; if he does, he falls.

Once again, to many, Zen may seem like a no-win situation. When actually Zen is a dilemma, where one has to take a decision and be prepared to face the consequences of that decision. Here taking the decision is as important as facing the consequences.

chapter 17

high energy diet in ZeNLP

A Zen prayer reads....

I asked for strength,
And God gave me difficulties to make me strong;
I asked for wisdom,
And God gave me problems to solve;
I asked for prosperity,
And God gave me brain and brawn to work;
I asked for courage,
And God gave me dangers to overcome;
I asked for love,
And God gave me troubled people to help;
I asked for favour,
And God gave me opportunities;
I received nothing I wanted,

but everything I needed;
My prayer has been answered.

There is a great truth hidden behind this simple prayer. Often in life we fail to recognise opportunities, and opportunity never knocks twice. ZeNLP recognises the fact that the mind and the body are parts of the same system. It also believes that the microcosm (body) and macrocosm (universe) are connected. There is a great opportunity to multiply our mind power manifold by following a Zen diet. This diet when followed by ZeNLP meditation improves concentration, memory and energy levels. It also boosts creativity, mind power and will power.

ZeNLP considers the following facts:

75 per cent of the earth is covered with water
75 per cent of the human body is composed of water

To maintain a balance between the microcosm and macrocosm, it is mandatory to consume foods that contain 70 per cent water, to ensure the success of ZeNLP visualisation, auto-suggestion and meditation. The diet prescribed at ZeNLP workshops is carefully analysed not only to ensure that it contains 70 per cent water but also to maintain the nutritional balance in terms of vitamins, minerals, proteins and calories.

The diet recommended for ZeNLP meditation is a Zen diet which is the strict, or pure, form of vegetarianism.

No animal products are consumed; it comprises only fruits, vegetables, nuts, dry fruits and sprouts. No eggs, cheese, yoghurt, ice cream, butter, or other milk products are eaten.

This diet is not suggested for children unless the parents can painstakingly oversee it and select the right foods. With this diet, it is difficult to obtain a balanced intake of all the nutrients that are needed during growth; however, it can be done. This is true also in pregnancy and lactation, where higher intakes of most nutrients are needed. I am not suggesting that this cannot be done; it may create deficiencies and subsequent health problems if not supervised by ZeNLP experts.

Overall, ZeNLPers who follow this diet, weekly once, often lose weight, have lower cholesterol levels and more Zenergy. There is a much lower incidence of hypertension, obesity, heart disease, and some cancers, most notably of the colon, breast, uterus, and prostate among ZeNLPers who follow this diet and meditation. The fibre content of the diet is usually very good. *Surya Namaskar* is prescribed for those who do not get adequate sunshine, to boost their Vitamin D levels. Dry fruits and nuts make up the protein, zinc and calcium content. Dates are a rich source of iron.

Overall, with the right intention and knowledge, the Zen diet may be a very healthy one but should be followed only once a week by beginners.

The ZeNLP diet

Starter:

Clear vegetable soup
and
Fresh fruit juice (Mousambi/Orange/Pineapple)

Main Course:

Boiled lentils (Kabuli Chana (White Gram), Rajma (Baked Beans), Brown Chana (Bengal Gram)
and
Boiled vegetables (Cauliflower, Beans, Capsicum, Green Peas)
and
Vegetable salad (Cucumber, Cabbage, Tomato, Spinach, Lettuce, Green Coriander)
and
Sprouts (Channa, Moong, Tuver)

Desert:

Dates
Bananas
Papayas
Apples
Assorted dry fruits (Cashew Nuts, Figs, Raisins, Almonds, Walnuts)

chapter 18

meditation in ZeNLP

Zen monks who practise meditation are physically healthier and mentally at peace. A point to note here is that these monks are strict vegans. Vegans are strict vegetarians who avoid milk and all milk products. Vegans also avoid eating honey. They do not wear leather, use leather goods and refrain from wearing silk or using any products of animal origin. Vegans do not eat any animal protein including eggs, fish, poultry and meat or any products directly or indirectly sourced from animals e.g. gelatine.

The most astounding fact about Zen meditation is that similar meditations are being practised by tribal societies in Africa, North America, Orissa, Dangs and Wynad.

Most of these tribals are untouched by modern medicine, yet are physically stronger, cheerful and more peaceful than their urban counterparts. The human mind is a powerful computer and computers can be programmed using software programs. Thus, the human mind too can be programmed using software. ZeNLP meditation is this software; software for the human mind.

Sit in a comfortable posture, gently close your eyelids. Roll your eyeball upwards and take three deep breaths. Now visualise a running mountain stream in your mind. Relax to the gurgling sounds of this stream. Do this for three to five minutes and your migraine will disappear. You need not pop a pill anymore.

Whenever you find yourself anxious, tense or stressful, this simple ZeNLP meditation technique will allow you to lead a relaxed and more peaceful life. The greatest advantage of Zen meditation is its simplicity. No external modern gadgets like cassettes or discs are required. All you need is space, time and yourself. ZeNLP meditation can be practised while travelling on a train or bus, while taking a bath or while brushing your teeth. It can be absorbed seamlessly into your daily routine and can become a habit and, as good habits are the key to success, this good habit will effortlessly propel you to lead a healthy and peaceful life.

Once you install this software in your mind, Zen meditation will become your universal medication. Once you practise ZeNLP meditation you will need fewer visits to your doctor and the chemist shop and in about eight to 12 months, you will need no allopathic medicines as you would have discovered the secret to lead a healthy, happy and more fulfilling life.

chapter 19

synchronicity in ZeNLP

There are some really strange coincidences between the assassination of Abraham Lincoln and John F. Kennedy. The facts are detailed below. Read them and then ask yourself if there really is a link between the killings.

Lincoln was elected to Congress in 1846. Kennedy was elected to Congress in 1946. Lincoln was elected President in 1860. Kennedy was elected in 1960. Andrew Johnson, who succeeded Lincoln, was born in 1808. Lyndon Johnson, who succeeded Kennedy, was born in 1908. John Wilkes Booth, who assassinated Lincoln, was born in 1839. Lee Harvey Oswald, who assassinated Kennedy, was born in 1939. The name Lee Harvey Oswald contains 15 letters. The name John Wilkes Booth contains 15 letters. The name Lincoln contains seven letters. The name Kennedy contains seven letters. Booth shot Lincoln in the theatre and fled to a warehouse. Oswald supposedly shot Kennedy from a warehouse and fled to a theatre. Both Presidents were shot in the head. Both were sitting beside their wives when they were shot. Both were killed on a Friday. Lincoln's secretary, named Kennedy, warned him not to go to the theatre. Kennedy's secretary, named Lincoln, warned him not to go to Dallas. Lincoln was shot and died in the Ford Theatre. Kennedy was shot and killed in a Ford automobile. And that automobile was a Lincoln. Both assassins were killed before being brought to trial. Lincoln and Kennedy were both directly concerned with Civil Rights. Booth and Oswald were both Southerners favouring unpopular ideas.

A mere coincidence? No American scientist has been able to provide a logical and scientific explanation for the links between the assassinations of these two Presidents.

However, it is possible to explain these startling coincidences in history by the spiritual laws of reincarnation and synchronicity. All events that happen in this universe are governed by the rules of synchronicity. There is a deep connection between seemingly unrelated events. This is part of a grand plan, in which we are mere participants.

After his death and subsequent burial, the molecules in Lincoln's body dissolved into the earth and became part of the earth's soil. These molecules were transferred into maize which grew on the fields. This maize was eaten by Kennedy's grandfather, passed on to Kennedy's father and resulted in the birth of John Kennedy exactly 100 years later. The molecules from Lincoln were now in Kennedy's body because of the cosmic principle of synchronicity in this universe.

The same laws of synchronicity ruled the lives of Lyndon Johnson, Andrew Johnson, Booth and Oswald. The coincidences between the lives of these two presidents were not mere coincidences but the execution of a grand plan by forces of nature. Kennedy had to keep his date with destiny, his secretary's warning notwithstanding.

How do managers at ZeNLP workshops benefit from this cosmic law of synchronicity? First, during the workshop, managers set their personal, family and career goals. Then they put down these goals in writing. The important point about their goal-setting exercises are:

1. Their goals have to be specific not vague
2. Their goals have to be measurable
3. Their goals have to be ambitious (neither too easy nor too difficult)
4. Their goals have to be realistic
5. They should specify a time-frame for reaching their goal

The minimum period for setting a short-term goal is five to 10 years. Second, they learn the ZeNLP visualisation techniques required to programme their unconscious mind to reach their goals faster. They also coin powerful self-affirmations about their goals and chant them like mantras. Mind power music cassettes (fire music for visuals, water music for auditories and earth music for kinesthetics) are given to participants at ZeNLP workshops. Managers need to play this tape in the background during self-affirmation exercises, which are to be done indoors.

Third, all participants plant a sapling during the workshop based on their preferred mental maps. Visuals plant Gulmohar saplings, auditories plant Ashoka saplings and kinesthetics plant Neem saplings.

Participants are expected to visit their saplings daily, remove their footwear and symbolically cup their hands with water and pour it on the sapling. This meditation can be done only during daylight. After watering their tree, participants have to face the sun, gently close their eyelids and visualise themselves reaching the goals they set for themselves at the workshop. These simple visualisations last for five to six minutes only.

This meditation can only be done on the days that participants have adhered to the vegan ZeNLP diet. For faster results, it is recommended that participants stick to the ZeNLP diet throughout their life. However, participants who have followed the ZeNLP diet, meditation, visualisation and, auto-suggestion once a week, have also reached their goals.

At home, participants play the music, repeat the auto-suggestions for five to six minutes thrice daily. Once each at dawn, noon and dusk. They also maintain a detailed dream diary, noting down their dreams every morning. Dreams are recorded in intricate detail and dates where they don't get dreams or don't remember their dreams are also marked in the dream diary record sheets. At the end of the month, the dream diaries are analysed. It is during the analysis of the dream diary that the cosmic law of synchronicity comes into play.

Managers who follow ZeNLP diet, meditation, visualisation, chanting, listen to ZeNLP music and maintain their dream diaries begin to experience mean-ingful coincidences. They begin to be guided by their infinite intelligence within them on the decisions and actions needed to reach their goal. Meaningful coinci-dences begin to happen.

Prashant attended our ZeNLP workshop in 1995 and was the export manager of a pharmaceutical company. Prashant had set his sights on becoming the vice-president (exports) of his company within five years. No mean achievement for a middle-level export manager. After a year of ZeNLP meditation he began seeing dreams about meeting his school classmate Priyadarshi who had migrated to Africa and whom he hadn't seen in over 30 years.

Once on a domestic flight from Ahmedabad to Banga-lore, the aircraft landed in Mumbai as it was a hopping flight. Prashant who was travelling in economy class, was upgraded to business class by Indian Airlines at Mumbai, to balance the load factor. Prashant had just nestled into his seat, when he saw his childhood friend Priyadarshi enter the aircraft and plonk himself down in the adjacent seat. By a meaningful coincidence, Priyadarshi was the purchase director of a South African drug distributor and had come to India looking to place a huge order for generics exactly what Prashant's company used to export. Needless to say this multi-crore contract became the turning point in Prashant's career. The business relationship between Prashant's and Priyadarshi's companies continued and Prashant was gradually elevated to vice-president (exports) by 2000.

Here is another example of the effect of the law of synchronicity.

We had been trying to conduct our ZeNLP based workshop at Paradip Port Trust since 1997. However, our efforts had yielded little or no results. I have been regularly maintaining and updating my dream diary since January 1995. I regularly analyse my dream diaries as the infinite intelligence of the cosmos reveals forthcoming events through the language of dreams. On January 1, 1998, I had recorded a dream in my dream diary where I had seen myself conducting ZeNLP meditation exercise on an isolated beach. I was guiding a team of 20 middle-aged couples on the seashore. In 1998, I was invited by Madras Management Association Chennai, State Bank Staff College, Hyderabad and Nalco, Bhubaneshwar to conduct introductory lectures on ZeNLP for their managers. I made my travel plans accordingly. From Ahmedabad, I flew to Hyderabad by the midnight flight. I finished my talk at Hyderabad and left by Falaknuma Express to Bhubhaneshwar. I completed my meeting at Nalco and rushed to catch the Coromandel Express to Chennai. I had only a few minutes to rush to the station after my lecture and the inevitable happened. I reached the station five minutes after the scheduled departure of the train, only to see the train leaving. I had given up hope, but due to a meaningful coincidence, the train slowed down and stopped. I rushed into the second A.C. coach and had barely managed to enter the compartment safely with my luggage, when the train started moving again. I could see a middle-aged man rushing towards the coach with his bag. I lent him a helping hand and he managed to enter the coach with my assistance. By the law of synchronicity, his seat was adjacent to mine. I introduced myself to this gentleman in the morning and soon I was friendly with Basant Kumar Satpathy, Chief Engineer at Paradip Port Trust! Satpathy was enroute to Bangalore through Chennai on a personal visit. Needless to say, we conducted a two day ZeNLP workshop for the senior managerial team of Paradip Port Trust and you guessed it right! The tree plantation meditation and ZeNLP meditation took place on an isolated beach at the port and most participants brought along their spouses for the Zen meditation session conducted on the seashore!

The mind is like a garden, if you sow seeds, nurture them with care and water it daily, you will see a thousand bejewelled red-hued rose-bushes bloom. Thus, if you set goals, nurture them with positive affirmations, water them with creative visualisation daily, you will see a thousand meaningful coincidences happen and the cosmic laws of synchronicity will guide you with their hidden hand and you will reach your goal unconsciously through little effort.

We realise the value of the laws of synchronicity and a scientific time-line analysis of the lives of participants at our ZeNLP workshops help them to set long-term goals in their careers. Most participants at our workshops have already reached goals they set themselves as early as 1995. The laws of synchronicity has made sure that the right coincidences at the right time, propel them to achieve their goals.

chapter 20

management lessons from penguins

No natural hazard that this planet offers can rival the circumstances assaulting the life expectancy of the emperor penguin's young. The emperor breeds only on the ice of the Antarctic continent. And he breeds in winter. When March comes, and the southern Autumn darkens, the emperor, his wife and his friends conduct their grave march inland across the ice to that place where tradition dictates that they must breed. There will be no nest of stones. She will lay her single egg on ice of fathomless depth, and he will pick the egg up on his foot. Then she will go away, back to the sea and their only source of food. He will remain with the egg on his foot. The perpetual night will enclose him. The

Antarctic winter will blow, shudder, sigh, snap, crush, and torment the present as it has tormented all ages. He will stand with the egg on his foot. He will stand very close among his friends as shoulder to shoulder they preserve their heat. There will be no argument, disputes over property, dominance, borders, prerogatives.

On rare occasions, the night will clear to reveal the Southern Cross in cruel arrangement. More often the storm will close down. All will vanish. There will be the wind and the cold beyond calculation. There will be the horror of nature's racket, and the horror of nature's silence. There will be the terror of nature's incredible blackness. There will be the terror of nature's soft illumination. And all the time the emperor penguin and his friends will be standing in a dense, unarguing mass, each with an egg on his foot, while slowly they revolve, presenting to this one the periphery of Antarctic hostility, presenting to that one a respite, a moment of comfort and warmth in the heartland of the social body.

For two months, this will be their dispensation. Then, their wives, fat and hearty, will return from the sea. The males will surrender their eggs, themselves seek the succour of wide-open waters, the freedom, the succulence of life. When they return, the chicks will have hatched. Springtime will be on its way, and the sunshine, and that is the most favourable season for the survival of the young. This, after all, was the whole evolutionary point, the reason for the time of winter trial.

Brooks too broad for leaping divide us from animal agony. Walls too tall for weeping contain our sympathies. We cannot, with presence human or divine, apprehend the living moment in a mass of male emperor penguins revolving each with an egg on his foot in a dark, frozen, endless Antarctic night beneath frigid, withdrawn, uncaring stars. You do not know, nor will you ever. I shall not know, nor shall I ever.

Observe nature with new eyes...

There is a very deep meaning and important lessons to be learnt from this true story of the Antarctic penguins. We managers are like the emperor penguins, are the guardians of our subordinates, facing the hostile environment of the highly competitive market.

We too, have an egg each on our foot, and are instinctively ensuring our survival in the corporate rat race. What can we learn from these Antarctic penguins?

Team-work

As the harsh winter winds blow over the icy Antarctic, the flock of penguins, huddle together to conserve their body heat. There is no better example of solidarity and team-work, where each penguin knows that the survival of their offsprings depends on their unity.

Organisations are nothing more than a collection of penguins who have come together to achieve a common goal or objective. In the face of severe competition, managers

should come together as a team and utilise their collective
wisdom to arrive at cutting-edge strategies which will ensure
their marketshares and growth rates in the marketplace.

Selflessness

As these penguins single-mindedly guard the eggs of
their offspring in the harsh Antarctic winter, they forget
their ego. Their ego takes a back-seat and all disputes
over property, borders and mates is forgotten. Each
penguin becomes a cog in the wheel, so that its evolutionary cycle continues.

Here lies a great lesson for us. Managers should forget old
rivalries like promotions, perks, salary differences and
seniority and become cogs in the wheel so that the organisation
meets its objectives.

Division of work

Just as the male penguins guard the egg on their foot
through the winter and the darkness, the female penguins go to the sea and collect food. And after the winter,
the well-fed female penguin returns to the egg and
hatches them.

Organisations should divide the work among managers
based on their skills and abilities.

All work is no fun

From these penguins we see that while the males guard
the egg on their foot through the severe winter, the

females enjoy their freedom, gather food and become healthy to return and hatch their eggs. Once the females return, it is the turn of the males, after facing the harshest of Antarctic winters, to have their turn at fun and frolic.

There is a very simple message for managers. Workaholism doesn't pay. It is essential for managers to relax and have fun in between bouts of strenuous work. A balance between hard work and fun is what keeps the Antarctic penguins clicking. Do not hesitate to take that long overdue vacation. Listen to foot-stomping music as you browse the Web. Take a break and attend that meditation workshop you have always wanted to.

chapter 21

management lessons from ants

Teams of mindless robots can achieve complex tasks without communicating with each other. Armies of such cheap, expendable robots might one day help build a base on Mars—or simply mow your lawn. Non-communicative behaviour in ants is observed when they combine their efforts to carry large bits of food such as leaves. Scientists have mimicked the same sort of distributed intelligence in a gang of worker robots. If you watch a particular ant, its behaviour seems chaotic and sometimes counterproductive, but the 'team' as a whole displays a form of intelligence despite the lack of central control.

This is an attractive lesson for scientists who build robots because such distributed systems tend to be very robust. It is a lot cheaper and easier to build a large number of simple robots than build one expensive complex robot to do the same job. A centrally-controlled system can be brought down by a single failure. An in-depth study of behaviour of ants reveal interesting results.

Although the behaviour of individual ants appears chaotic, ants constitute an orderly social structure with these various responses, lead a life based on mutual news exchange and they have no difficulty in achieving this correspondence. We could say that ants, with their impressive communication system, are 100 per cent successful on subjects that human beings sometimes cannot resolve nor agree upon by talking (e.g. meeting, sharing, cleaning, defence, etc.).

First, scout ants go to the food source that has been newly discovered. Then they call other ants by a liquid they secrete in their glands called pheromone. When the crowd round the food gets bigger, this pheromone secretion issues the workers a limit again. If the piece of food is very small or faraway, the scouts make an adjustment in the number of ants trying to get to the food by issuing signals. If a nice piece of food is found, the ants try harder to leave more traces, thus more ants from the nest come to the aid of the foragers. Whatever happens, no problems arise in the consumption of the food and its transportation to the nest, because what we have here is perfect 'team work'.

What can we learn from these foraging ants?

Team work

Ants are perfect team players and sacrifice their individual ambitions to become cogs in a wheel in order to ensure the evolutionary progress of their species.

Balance

Just as the pheromone secretion ensures the correct balance of ants, ensuring effective and efficient transport of food, managers who balance work with play are cheerful, relaxed and successful.

Discipline

Just as the army of ants are disciplined in their approach and go about their task with one mind, managers who are disciplined and dedicated are more likely to be successful leaders.

chapter 22
management lessons from dolphins

No other mammal has captivated human imagination as the playful dolphin. Close observations of dolphin behaviour reveal interesting truths. Dolphins are playful and seem to know how to enjoy living. They do fine on their own but do even better when they swim or work in a group. There are many instances of a group of dolphins protecting humans against sharks and assisting drowning sailors. Dolphins have a tremendous healing effect on humans and as they are neither overly aggressive nor overly passive, dolphins are able to live in balance within the ocean's domain. There is some evidence that their nervous system is more complex than humans and their brains bigger than ours, so this could mean that they are actually more advanced than we are as a species!

When dolphins are travelling, their movements are usually synchronised. They dive together and they come up to the surface to breathe together. Dolphins can be active both night and day. A large part of their activity pattern is dictated by the food they eat. In some areas, dolphins are more active at night and rest more during the day. On average, dolphins sleep about eight hours every 24 hours. Their sleeping behaviour is different from our own. When people sleep, the whole brain displays a sleeping pattern. In dolphins, only one half of the brain sleeps at any given time. The brain hemispheres take turns in sleeping.

The bond between mothers and their calves is strong. Calves stay with their mothers for a long time, usually three to six years, but sometimes even longer. Even later in life, dolphins occasionally associate with their mothers, although usually only briefly. When the calves leave they join sub-adult groups. These sub-adult groups are quite active. In these groups, the young dolphins learn how to behave in a group and where a hierarchy will be established. Females in the same reproductive condition will group together: Females that are pregnant, or females with calves of approximately the same age. Often, two or three males form a tight bond. Such a bond may develop when the animals are still sub-adults and it may persist for a long time.

Dolphins do work together. One of the most spectacular examples is found in dolphins in the Mississippi delta, who as a group chase a school of fish onto the river bank and then follow the fish onto the bank and grab the fish out of the water.

What can present day managers learn from these playful dolphins?

Synchronicity

Just as a group of dolphins demonstrate perfect synchronised swimming, managers who work together are no different from these dolphins and have to be in perfect physical, mental and spiritual synchronicity to effectively and efficiently achieve organisational goals and objectives. Individual activity has to be perfectly synchronised to achieve team goals.

Team work

Managers have to work as a team and employ strategies to beat competition just like the dolphins of the Missisipi Delta, who outsmart their prey through effective team work.

Groups

Groups of managers of similar age groups and social backgrounds work better in smaller teams of three to four members, as demonstrated by the bonding between pregnant female dolphins.

Social responsibility

Just as dolphins go out of their way to protect humans from sharks and save drowning sailors, managers must also include social responsibility in their working life.

Trust

Just as the dolphins who form bonds during sub-adulthood, continue to stay together for life, customers who develop bonds with your organisation when they are young, usually remain life-long customers.

Rest and playfulness

Adequate sleep and the right amount of playfulness are secret recipes for success.

chapter 23

management lessons
from gulls

A lot of lessons in management can be learnt if we simply keep our eyes open and observe. This is one of the most important aspects of continuous learning: Like when I saw a flock of birds flying in a perfect V formation. Nature has given these birds the instinct to help one another by flying in formation.

Each bird remains at the same distance from its neighbour, always a little to one side of the left or right wing of the bird in front. In this way, only the leading bird has to make a great effort to surmount the resistance of the air; the others take advantage of the currents from its wings, and so advance with less fatigue, each one helping the next.

From time to time another bird overtakes the leader and relieves it of its arduous task. These Canada Geese migrate to Britain for the winter from Greenland, Iceland and Arctic Russia. They are known to cover the distance from Iceland to Britain in one flight. They generally fly at a speed of around 40 miles an hour, so, assuming no wind, a goose will cover the 600 miles to Northern Britain in about 15 hours of non-stop flight, enabled to do this by flying in formation.

- What can we learn from these flying geese and how can these lessons benefit managers?

Every organisation is like these flying geese with one single aim, knowing where they are going and determined to get there, everyone of the same mind and realising how important each of us is to the rest. Team work is the key ingredient for organisational success.

- As each bird flaps its wings, it creates an 'uplift' for the bird immediately following. By flying in a 'V' formation, the whole flock has at least 71 per cent greater flying range than if each bird flew on its own.

Employees who share a common direction and sense of community can get where they are going more quickly and easily because they are travelling on the thrust of one another.

- When a goose flies out of formation, it suddenly feels the drag and resistance of trying to go it alone.

It quickly gets back into formation to take advantage of the lifting power of the bird in front of it.

If we have as much common sense as a goose, we stay in formation with those headed where we want to go. We are willing to accept their help and give our help to others. It is harder to do something alone than together.

- When the lead goose gets tired, it rotates back into formation and another goose flies to the point position.

It is sensible to take turns doing the hard and demanding tasks and sharing leadership. As with geese, people are interdependent of each other's skills, capabilities, and unique arrangements of gifts, talents, or resources.

- The geese flying in formation honk from behind to encourage those up front to keep up their speed.

We need to make sure our honking is encouraging. In groups where there is encouragement, the production is much greater. The power of encouragement (to stand by one's heart or core values and encourage the heart and core of others) is the quality of honking we seek. We need to make sure our honking is encouraging.

chapter 24

management lessons from owls

On March 22, 1997, Japan Railways launched commercial service of the 500-Series Shinkansen electric train with the co-operation of several railway rolling stock manufacturers. This train is one of the fastest in the world and has a top speed of 300 kmph. The train shortened the travelling time between Shin-Osaka and Tokyo—a distance of 1076 km—to just 4 hours and 49 minutes. No mean achievement even for a bullet train.

This achievement is attributable to the fruits of the running tests conducted by Japan Railways with its high-speed experimental electric cars, 'WIN350.' Extensive tests were conducted between 1992 and 1995. The main subject of developing the 500-Series train was not just how to make it run faster, but how to make it run more quietly. Then, Nakatsu Eiji one of the design engineers of the project, who was also an ornithologist, made a presentation to the top brass of Japan Railways about what he had learnt from the flying methods of wild birds.

Flight of an owl and low-noise Shinkansen electric trains

The goals of the railway engineers were tough. 'Safety' was ranked first. The second priority was to clear the environmental standards of Japan (prescribed by the Environment Agency in 1975), which prescribe the world's strictest noise standard for railway operators. Due to the development of current technologies, it was not so difficult to run the trains at high speed.

What was really tough was to run it more quietly. Under the prescribed standards, noise levels at a point 25 metres away from the centre of the railway track in urban areas had to be kept at 75 dB(A) or less (measured at normal conditions). As those who observe noise at a crossing in a town may notice, a noise level of 75 dB(A) means a fairly quiet atmosphere; a sonometer at a crossing easily exceeds 80 dB(A) when automobiles start moving all at once at the green light. This was one of the most important challenges that this group of railway engineers faced.

At lower speeds, the principal source of sound in the Shinkansen train is the rolling noise, which is generated from the kinetic contact between wheels and rails. The intensity of sound source is proportional to the square of the train speed. When it runs at high speeds at over 200 kmph, however, the sound source is the aerodynamic noise, which is proportional to the sixth of the train speed. In the electric cars, the aerodynamic noise is mostly produced by pantographs, or current collectors, that receive electricity from the overhead catenary. Realising that there would be limits to noise reduction by using the conventional pantographs that look exactly like two rectangular timbers put in parallel, the Japanese engineers set their hand to developing a wing-shaped pantograph, making a thorough investigation of the wings of birds. This revolutionary new idea was put forward by Eiji, the ornithologist.

In May 1990, at an indoor regular meeting of the Japan Wild Bird Association held at its Osaka branch, Eiji was taught by Yajima Seiichi, an association member and then an aircraft design engineer, that the owl family flies in the most silent manner among fowls. This is a wisdom ordained by nature that enables an owl to swoop down silently on a field mouse. One of the secrets of the owl family's low-noise flight lies in the plumes of the wings. There are many small saw-toothed feathers, which ordinary birds do not have, that stick out from the outer rim of the primaries. The saw-toothed wave feathers, generate small vortices in the air flow.

Aerodynamic noise is a sound generated by the vortices, which are produced in the air flow. The bigger the vortices grow, the more the noise. If you provide wings with many infinitesimally small saw-toothed projections, small vortices will be generated instead of big vortices. Thereupon, it is likely that the air resistance lessens and the aerodynamic noise decreases. This is a cogent explanation for the near-silent flight by owls.

Later, the Japanese Railway engineers conducted wind tunnel tests using a flight by a stuffed owl with the courtesy of the Osaka Municipal Tennoji Zoo. The result fell considerably short of their expectations, and they thought for a while that the case of an owl flying at 70 kmph or so could not be adopted to the Shinkansen running at such a high-speed as 300 kmph, and were about to give up the testing. Simultaneously, they found difficulty in developing the wing-shaped pantographs to conquer the aerodynamic lift. A wing exists to float like an aeroplane. However, if a pantograph had a very strong aerodynamic lift, it would push up the overhead catenary too much. That was also a problem. This subject was resolved by the partial re-shaping of the wing-shaped timber at the suggestion of Miyamura Motohiro, who was an association member and then a staff member of ANA (All Nippon Airways) Aircraft Maintenance and who had participated in this project having been introduced by Yajima Seichi. Then, they made a wing-shaped pantograph on an experimental basis for the first time in the world, and succeeded in the test runs at 320 kmph.

However, it was recognised through wind tunnel tests that the support of a wing-shaped pantograph also generates noise. In order to reduce the noise generated by the support, the Japanese engineers adopted the principle of the owl family's serrations and could efficiently reduce noise. The optimum cross-sectional shape of the above-mentioned vortex generators and, their fitting-up positions were determined by the young engineers through their strenuous and unremitting efforts. Japan Railways could foresee the possibility of fully satisfying the environmental standards with its Shinkansen trains in the range of 300 kmph hour or more, using wing-shaped pantographs. Other high speed train manufacturers like TGV of France are modifying their designs based on lessons learnt by Japan Railways from the flight of owls.

In ZeNLP workshops, we recognise the fact that nature manages 6 billion humans in addition to billions of animals, birds and trees. Nature is guided by infinite wisdom which has evolved over the ages. Hence, we learn management from hundreds of such examples of owls, gulls, penguins and eagles. These lessons help to increase the efficiency and effectiveness of managers to perform better in their designated role.

chapter 25

management lessons
from trees

The contingency theory says that management is what managers do. Researchers studied the activities of managers and came to the conclusion that as managers spend most of their time planning, organising, controlling and developing, the science of management was subdivided into these four activities. However these researchers missed out a vital truth and that is 'The whole is more than the sum of the parts.' Management is more of an art and less of a science as can be proved from the experience of hundreds of successful entrepreneurs who had no scientific training in management and many of whom built up Fortune 500 companies after starting out in their garages. Many successful entrepreneurs in India had little or no primary education and today, they manage companies with workforces that run into thousands. How do these managers succeed? The experiences that we remember the most are also the ones that are simple!

Management can be learnt by keenly observing nature. Children learn an incredible amount because they are open and unbiased. A child can play with a stick in total delight and all the while the child is learning—learning to move and to co-ordinate herself. She can watch the same movie over and over and still shudder with delight, still shiver with fear, and laugh with abandon—even though she knows what is coming. Children are learning sponges until they are trained to behave like young adults and are confined to desks and told to act appropriately. While adults look for the payoff, kids simply learn for the sheer pleasure it brings them. As adults, we need to recapture the sense of joy and adventure we had as children, to rekindle a sense of growing and contributing. Thus, the first lesson in management is that a manager must be like a child and learn continuously from his experiences.

Let us learn management from nature. It is easy and it is fun. A successful manager must be like a sandalwood tree. The same saw which cuts the sandalwood tree becomes fragrant due to the magnanimity of the sandalwood tree. Thus, in situations where managers have been victims of office politics, it is better to forgive and forget rather than harbour grudges, which could have devastating effects in the long run.

- A successful manager is also like a river. Just as the river starts as a small mountain stream between rocky crevices in the mountains, flows down the plains with a clear destination in mind and triumphantly merges into the ocean at the end, managers should also have a clear goal in mind, right from the planning stage. They have to accept the good with the bad but continue to flow in single-minded pursuit of their goal.

- A successful manager is like a ripe mango. Just as a ripe mango hangs heavy as it matures, managers should mellow with experience and as they rise in the hierarchy; it pays to be humble rather than be egoistic.

- A successful manager is like the ocean. Just as the ocean does not swell up after heavy rains, neither does it dry after long summer spells owing to its vastness and depth, managers should neither flare up nor be extremely docile while taking decisions but must attempt to seek a balance between discipline and freedom.

- A successful manager is like the ant. Just as the ant toils in the good months storing foodgrain for days of scarcity, managers should also conserve resources and finances in anticipation of leaner days. The dotcoms that have survived the shakeout in India like tips4ceos.com are the ones which conserved their resources during the boom.

about the author

Murli Menon is the President of phenoMenon consultants inc, Ahmedabad, which conducts mind power
development workshops for senior managers based on
Indian, Buddhist, Zen and Tibetan scriptures. These are
often weeklong workshops on mind power development
which are attended by senior management, company
directors and CEOs. Conceptualised and conducted by
Murli, these workshops are result oriented with a focus
on goal setting and achievement using creative
visualisation, dynamic meditation and ancient Vedic,
Egyptian, Mayan and Aztec mind power development
ceremonies. phenoMenon's clients include corporations
like Gujarat Narmada Valley Fertilizer Company (GNFC),
NCPL, AEC, Indian Telephone Industries (ITI), Paradeep
Port Trust (PPT), Strides Arcolab, Hindustan Aeronau-
tics Ltd. (HAL), Recon Healthcare, Trident Group and
Zydus Cadila among numerous others.

Murli holds a bachelors degree in biochemistry and an MBA with a specialisation in marketing from Institute for Management Development and Research (IMDR), Pune. He is currently engaged in advanced research on the effects of Zen Meditation on the unconscious mind and conducts ZeNLP workshops for students, teachers, housewives and corporates. Apart from his consultancy work, Murli has been a visiting faculty to many well known management institutes where he teaches product management, market research, sales management and direct marketing. Before founding phenoMenon consultants inc., Murli worked as a Product Manager with leading multinationals including Astra-IDL Ltd.

Murli is also a linguistic expert, a poet, and a storywriter. His articles on ZeNLP regularly appear in *Daily Shipping Times* and his research papers have also been published in *Saket, Human Capital, Pharma Trendz, Kasturi, Deccan Herald, Panorama, fe Business Traveller* and *Times of India* among numerous others. Murli's poems have been published in many national and international poetry journals. He is also the author of an anthology of poems titled *Environment Friendly Poetry*. Murli's autobiographical stories have been extensively published in various magazines. His work is also featured on numerous internet sites and he can be contacted over email at zenlp@rediffmail.com